WORLD HARVEST SCHOOL OF CONTINUOUS LEARNING

WORLD FAMILY
TARGETED FOR DEATH

LESTER SUMRALL

P.O. Box 12, South Bend, IN 46624

This special study guide is a college workbook. The space prepared for your personal notes is for the text to grow into your own material. Audio and Videotapes are also available.

Copyright All Rights Reserved
Printed, March 1992

THE WORLD FAMILY TARGETED FOR DEATH
Copyright © by Lester Sumrall Evangelistic Association
ISBN No. 0-937580-72-4

Printed by LESEA PUBLISHING CO.
P.O. Box 12
South Bend, Indiana 46624

STUDY GUIDE

WORLD HARVEST SCHOOL OF CONTINUOUS LEARNING

THE WORLD FAMILY TARGETED FOR DEATH

INDEX

Lesson	Page
Dedication	5
1. The Home—Targeted For Death	6
2. The Birth Of The World Family	11
3. The Meaning Of Marriage	14
4. The Three Worlds Of Marriage	18
5. The Right Relationship Between Man And Woman	21
6. Unfaithfully Yours (Hosea's Wife)	24
7. Demon Spirits Break Up Homes	28
8. Who Wants To Destroy The World Home?	31
9. Seven Women And One Man	34
10. What Jesus Taught Concerning Marriage	44
11. How To Stay Married	46
12. Ten Family Hurdles	50
13. Ten Principals Of Marital Bliss	52
14. Deadly Destroyers Of The World Home	55
15. Protecting Your Home From Family And Friends	57
16. The Greatest Mother-In-Law	59
17. The Unfaithful Father-In-Law	63
18. The King Makes Love To A Stepdaughter	67

STUDY GUIDE

WORLD HARVEST SCHOOL OF CONTINUOUS LEARNING

THE WORLD FAMILY—TARGETED FOR DEATH

DEDICATION

This syllabus is dedicated to the endtime leaders. Matthew 19:4-6, *And he answered and said unto them, Have ye not read, that he which made them at the beginning made them male and female, and said, For this cause shall a man leave father and mother, and shall cleave to his wife: and they twain shall be one flesh? Wherefore they are no more twain, but one flesh. What therefore God hath joined together, let not man put asunder.*

STUDY GUIDE

WORLD HARVEST SCHOOL OF CONTINUOUS LEARNING

THE WORLD FAMILY—TARGETED FOR DEATH

Lesson 1

THE HOME—TARGETED FOR DEATH

INTRODUCTION:

Our subject of study is the home. The home is being targeted for death by most of modern society. The purpose of this teaching session is for you and I to understand how to consolidate and save the human home.

We believe it is much easier to have a happy home through a knowledge of Christ. However, we do know it is possible for humans to live together peaceably anywhere in the world, under any conditions.

The oldest continuously active organization among men is what we call the home. The first institution ever to be upon planet Earth was the establishment we called the home. For some 6,000 years, the home has been ecumenical—the all-embracing cement that holds society together, place of desire, where we cleave together, fighting our enemies as a unit.

1. **THE HOME UNDER ATTACK**

    This organism called home, with its dynamic energy, is the most tried institution in the history of mankind and, in our generation, is TARGETED FOR DEATH. Later, we will examine who wants to destroy the home and why. Through the ages, many hateful attempts have been made to fragment the home and through it, destroy the human family. There is total hate in high-ranking organizations that do not believe the teachings of the Word of God. They seek to inject a venomous poison into the home, causing the disintegration of that which has been cemented together by love, promise and covenant.

2. **THIS CENTURY HAS ATTACKED THE HOME**

    Our century could be remembered as the one century which targeted the family, to tear it from its foundations and see civilization annihilated because of the destruction of the greatest institution man has ever known—the home.

    A. World Wars

The Home—Targeted For Death
Lesson 1, Page 2

In our century, we have had the two greatest wars, called World War I and World War II. Following World War II, we saw the greatest attack against the home in all the history of mankind. We had lived generation after generation after generation with many things falling to pieces, but the home held together. However since these two great wars, the home has suffered more than any other institution. Why? Could it be prophetic that these are the Last Days? Or could it mean that we have disjointed the home by its members going their own way, and we haven't taken time to rebuild the structure of the home.

B. Civil Wars

Not only have we had two world wars, we have actually seen hundreds of civil wars all over the face of this earth in this century. At this very minute in various parts of the world, civil wars are destroying the home. They knock down the houses. They decimate the men, and the women have no one to care for them. The children become victims and orphans. The wars of the world have done a lot in destroying the beautiful home.

C. Domestic Wars

The home has suffered from many aspects of what we call "modern" civilization, maybe more than any other system. Millions of women and mothers left the home and went into world commerce, the market place, for employment. The home no longer had the almost irresistible love flowing from it on a continual all-day basis.

D. Social Wars

The place of respect and reverence that was once the home has been torn apart by such things as Communism, Nazism, and Fascism. China, which built the largest society the world has ever known with one race and one government, has violently changed from when I visited it many years ago. It is no longer ruled by the head of the house as it was in those days, but is now ruled by the government. In our land, humanism has attacked the home to cause it to cease to possess the force and power it had been in other generations.

3. THE SEAT OF STRENGTH

The seat or throne of strength of the human race is the cementing together of units who swore allegiance of faithfulness and fidelity "till death do us part." The core of the foundation of society is when the male and female desire to cohabit and, in allegiance, covenant together under God and declare that "forsaking all others, for you and you alone..." This covenant of blood unites the male and female into bonds of reproducing another generation. When this is in our hearts and in our souls, God can bless a home.

4. NO PLACE LIKE HOME

Society's great pyramid of strength is not the monumental correctional institutions of courts and prisons. Man's greatest fortitude is not in his palaces of justice, where esteemed chief judges fabricate and enunciate precepts of human conduct.

The Home—Targeted For Death
Lesson 1, Page 3

The highest tower of global strength, the very cement that holds the collective body of Homo sapiens in the unity of the society of men, IS THE HOME. It is true...there is no place like home!

5. THE FAMILY IS DIVINE

Genesis 2:18, 21-23, *And the LORD God said, It is not good that the man should be alone; I will make him an help meet for him.*

v. 21, *And the LORD God caused a deep sleep to fall upon Adam, and he slept: and he took one of his ribs, and closed up the flesh instead thereof;*

v. 22, *And the rib, which the LORD God had taken from man, made he a woman, and brought her unto the man.*

v. 23, *And Adam said, This is now bone of my bones, and flesh of my flesh: she shall be called Woman, because she was taken out of Man.*

6. WHY DOES A GOOD AND SUCCESSFUL FAMILY BEGIN AT MARRIAGE?

The early training a child receives in the family is either building future family success or the deadly evils of sorrow and family destruction.

7. YOUTH AND THE HOME

Some youth are fully ready for family disruption and divorce, even before they are married.

8. ABRAHAM AND HIS FAMILY

I studied how God wanted a family to stay together from the Bible. God said of Abraham in Genesis 18:19, *For I know him, that he will command his children and his household after him, and they shall keep the way of the LORD, to do justice and judgment; that the LORD may bring upon Abraham that which he hath spoken of him.*

9. LOT AND HIS FAMILY

Lot, Abraham's nephew, did not bring up his family correctly and his children were left with nothing but a bad memory. His daughters married Sodomites. His rebellious wife looked back and was turned into salt.

Genesis 19:14, 26, *And Lot went out, and spake unto his sons in law, which married his daughters, and said, Up, get you out of this place; for the LORD will destroy this city. But he seemed as one that mocked unto his sons in law.*

v. 26, *But his wife looked back from behind him, and she became a pillar of salt.*

The Home—Targeted For Death
Lesson 1, Page 4

10. FATHERS AND FAMILIES

Men must never shirk their share of family discipline. As a father, he must be fatherly, not disciplining in anger. His potential strength is not necessarily physical, but positive, with full purpose, and an explanation of why punishment is necesssary. It could be the denying of privileges, enjoyments, money, cars, games, etc.

11. MOTHERS MUST BE STRONG

A mother has a tremendous responsibility to her husband first and then to her children. Her life is closely associated with the children. She is the spiritual cohesion that holds the family structure together.

12. GARDEN OF EDEN

It was in the bliss of the Garden of Eden that the Elohim God made the family of man. Man was given dominion over everything that moves. He was king.

Genesis 1:26, *And God said, Let us make man in our image, after our likeness: and let them have dominion over the fish of the sea, and over the fowl of the air, and over the cattle, and over all the earth, and over every creeping thing that creepeth upon the earth.*

13. ADAM NEEDED A HELP MEET

In this place of divine perfection, God discovered that Adam's greatest need, in his solitary dominion over everything that moves on planet Earth, was a woman. Even in Paradise, something was lacking. God said it was a woman. Therefore, God created Eve to be a help meet to Adam. Now there were two. . . it was a family!

14. THE FIRST FAMILY

To be number one! The first family. What a happy family it was! They had a wonderful home with no pests, no pain, no volcanoes and no earthquakes. The first family was a fulfilled family.

15. THE LESTER AND LOUISE SUMRALL FAMILY

A. Louise and I have not suffered a major confrontation of anger, of spite, or of abusing each other by word or deed, in our nearly 50 years of marriage. For this reason, we have a right to speak on this subject.

B. Honeymoon

Louise and I have lived in circumstances conducive to conflict. On our honeymoon, we traveled up the Amazon River for 1,200 miles in terrible tropical heat. We slept in hammocks because there were no beds. We ate disagreeable food in the jungles. But primitive life did not destroy our love.

The Home—Targeted For Death
Lesson 1, Page 5

    C. The lost accordion—Later, in Sao Paulo State, Brazil, we sold Louise's personal accordion, which she played for our special music and singing in our crusades, for travel money. Louise never uttered a whimper of despair. Our love covered the lost property.

    D. Pots and pans—In the Republic of the Philippines, I sold Louise's stainless kitchenware pots and pans, to help pay for the production of a documentary missionary film. We had brought these beautiful pots and pans from America.

    E. War—When our family was living in Israel, we were caught in the Sinai War. I wanted to stay in Jerusalem throughout the war and Louise agreed. We had three small sons with us. We painted all our apartment windows black for the air raids and told our sons we would be safe, for God would keep us. There was no panic and no fear.

    F. We have founded and built churches together in Hong Kong, the Philippines and America. We have had to believe God for large amounts of money. Louise never let unbelief in God or me get to her. She believed God with me for miracles. Because of such varied experiences, we have a right to teach these truths.

16. WHO MAKES A SUCCESSFUL MARRIAGE? EVERY MAN AND WOMAN

    A. I believe that marital happiness is created by you!

    B. I believe that happiness is an achievement.

    C. For sure, living happy is not accidental.

    D. This means that marital happiness is purposeful, and I believe that the apex of human happiness is the human family.

17. LIVING "HAPPY" EVER AFTER

    A. Living happy ever after is the incredible survival story of the human family's life together. No institution on planet Earth has been so tested, so attacked, so abused as the human family.

    B. Tyranny has risen against the family from its inception. The devil has hurled polygamy, incest, lust, male and female perversion, divorce and even death to destroy the family.

STUDY GUIDE

WORLD HARVEST SCHOOL OF CONTINUOUS LEARNING

THE WORLD FAMILY—TARGETED FOR DEATH

Lesson 2

THE BIRTH OF THE WORLD FAMILY

INTRODUCTION:

Why did God create man? It was to bestow Divine love upon an object of His creation.

Psalm 8:4-9, *What is man, that thou art mindful of him? and the son of man, that thou visitest him?*

v. 5, *For thou hast made him a little lower than the angels, and hast crowned him with glory and honour.*

v. 6, *Thou madest him to have dominion over the works of thy hands; thou hast put all things under his feet:*

v. 7, *All sheep and oxen, yea, and the beasts of the field;*

v. 8, *The fowl of the air, and the fish of the sea, and whatsoever passeth through the paths of the seas.*

v. 9, *O LORD our Lord, how excellent is thy name in all the earth!*

READING:

Genesis 2:7, 15, 18, 21-24, *And the LORD God formed man of the dust of the ground, and breathed into his nostrils the breath of life; and man became a living soul.*

v. 15, *And the LORD God took the man, and put him into the garden of Eden to dress it and to keep it.*

v. 18, *And the LORD God said, It is not good that the man should be alone; I will make him an help meet for him.*

v. 21, *And the LORD God caused a deep sleep to fall upon Adam, and he slept: and he took one of his ribs and closed up the flesh instead thereof;*

v. 22, *And the rib, which the LORD God had taken from man, made he a woman, and brought her unto the man.*

The Birth Of The World Family
Lesson 2, Page 2

v. 23, And Adam said, This is now bone of my bones, and flesh of my flesh: she shall be called Woman, because she was taken out of Man.

v. 24, Therefore shall a man leave his father and his mother, and shall cleave unto his wife: and they shall be one flesh.

1. **FIRST THINGS ARE GLAMOROUS**

    A. First car

    B. First home

    C. The birth of the human family. Our Father God, who already understood family meanings, established the home.

2. **GOD CREATED MAN: STRONG AND BEAUTIFUL, BUT ALONE**

    Man did not come from a slime pit, he came from the hand of God. Even with Eden's bounty and beauty, there was a lack. Adam had one need. He needed a help meet that the fauna or flora could not supply—a companion.

3. **GOD MADE A WOMAN**

    God took her from a part of man for man to be fulfilled. The man and woman had different bodies, minds, emotions, and wills.

4. **GOD UNITED THEM TOGETHER AND CALLED IT MARRIAGE**

    Through their children, they became one. God said, "The two shall be one."

    God also said, "What God hath joined together, let no man put asunder."

    God said, "Forsaking all others for her."

    A man must leave father and mother for his wife.

    Genesis 2:24, *Therefore shall a man leave his father and his mother, and shall cleave unto his wife: and they shall be one flesh.*

5. **ADAM AND EVE BECAME THE FIRST HUMAN FAMILY**

    A. Their first children were two sons.

        Genesis 4:1-2, *And Adam knew Eve his wife; and she conceived, and bare Cain, and said, I have gotten a man from the LORD.*

        v. 2, *And she again bare his brother Abel. And Abel was a keeper of sheep, but Cain was a tiller of the ground.*

The Birth Of The World Family
Lesson 2, Page 3

B. Cain and Abel were the first earth-born children. They were a family of four living together.

C. Death came by murder, resulting from anger and hate.

Genesis 4:3-8, *And in process of time it came to pass, that Cain brought of the fruit of the ground an offering unto the LORD.*

v. 4, *And Abel, he also brought of the firstlings of his flock and of the fat thereof. And the LORD had respect unto Abel and to his offering:*

v. 5, *But unto Cain and to his offering he had not respect. And Cain was very wroth, and his countenance fell.*

v. 6, *And the LORD said unto Cain, Why art thou wroth? and why is thy countenance fallen?*

v. 7, *If thou doest well, shalt thou not be accepted? and if thou doest not well, sin lieth at the door. And unto thee shall be his desire, and thou shalt rule over him.*

v. 8, *And Cain talked with Abel his brother: and it came to pass, when they were in the field, that Cain rose up against Abel his brother, and slew him.*

Earth's first family found itself in a great disruption. They refused the divine pattern, they walked the road of rebellion.

STUDY GUIDE

WORLD HARVEST SCHOOL OF CONTINUOUS LEARNING

THE WORLD FAMILY—TARGETED FOR DEATH

Lesson 3

THE MEANING OF MARRIAGE

INTRODUCTION:

When a young man marries a young woman, a family is born. The most intimate of human relationships is a marriage of one man to one woman.

READING:

Proverbs 18:22, *Whoso findeth a wife findeth a good thing, and obtaineth favour of the LORD.*

Ecclesiastes 9:9, *Live joyfully with the wife whom thou lovest all the days of the life of thy vanity, which he hath given thee under the sun, all the days of thy vanity: for that is thy portion in this life, and in thy labour which thou takest under the sun.*

Ephesians 5:33, *Nevertheless let every one of you in particular so love his wife even as himself; and the wife see that she reverence her husband.*

Malachi 2:15, *And did not he make one? Yet had he the residue of the spirit. And wherefore one? That he might seek a godly seed. Therefore take heed to your spirit, and let none deal treacherously against the wife of his youth.*

1. **THE BLOOD COVENANT**

   The male and female mix blood and create an immortal soul. When my natural life began, I soon learned:

   A. I am a male, I was born that way.

   B. I learned what a male is and what makes him different than a female.

   C. I learned that my mother was female and that my father was male. I learned this early in babyhood.

   D. I learned that my older and younger sisters, Louise, Anna and Leona, were female.

The Meaning Of Marriage
Lesson 3, Page 2

    E. I learned that my brothers, Ernest, Houston and Kerney, all older, were male.

    F. I soon understood males more easily than females.

    G. I dressed like a male and became accustomed to it.

    H. I learned that males had a specific toilet in public places and not to get them mixed up!

2. I FURTHER LEARNED THAT A MALE HAS SEVERAL VERY DISTINCT RELATIONS WITH FEMALES

    A. A mother: To love and obey her who gave you birth, fed and clothed you.

    B. A sister: If older, she cared for you.

    C. An aunt: She was the sister of your father or mother.

    D. A grandmother: She was the mother of your father or mother.

    E. A wife: Adam first knew Eve as an adult and he was a mature man.

    F. A daughter: She was a jewel from heaven.

3. OTHER RELATIONSHIPS WITH FEMALES

Besides this natural relationship with females, there are spiritual relationships.

    A. A mother in the faith—one who can counsel.

    B. A sister in Christ—a fellow member of the church.

4. RESPECT MUST BE SHOWN

I learned that respect was commanded for all of them, but sex is forbidden with most of them.

    A. Near of kin.

    Leviticus 18:6, *None of you shall approach to any that is near of kin to him, to uncover their nakedness: I am the LORD.*

    B. Mother or Father

    Leviticus 18:7-8, *The nakedness of thy father, or the nakedness of thy mother, shalt thou not uncover: she is thy mother; thou shalt not uncover her nakedness.*

    v. 8, *The nakedness of thy father's wife shalt thou not uncover: it is thy father's nakedness.*

    C. Sister

    Leviticus 18:9, *The nakedness of thy sister, the daughter of thy father, or daughter of thy mother, whether she be born at home, or born abroad, even their nakedness thou shalt not uncover.*

The Meaning Of Marriage
Lesson 3, Page 3

- **D.** Stepsister (half-sister)

    Leviticus 18:11, *The nakedness of thy father's wife's daughter, begotten of thy father, she is thy sister, thou shalt not uncover her nakedness.*

- **E.** Granddaughter

    Leviticus 18:10, *The nakedness of thy son's daughter, or of thy daughter's daughter, even their nakedness thou shalt not uncover: for theirs is thine own nakedness.*

- **F.** Daughter-in-law

    Leviticus 18:15, *Thou shalt not uncover the nakedness of thy daughter in law: she is thy son's wife; thou shalt not uncover her nakedness.*

- **G.** Sister-in-law

    Leviticus 18:16, *Thou shalt not uncover the nakedness of thy brother's wife: it is thy brother's nakedness.*

5. **I GREW UP AND LEARNED THE WONDER OF A FAMILY**

    A. We ate at one table.

    B. We helped each other in work and play.

    C. We stuck together in times of trouble.

    D. I learned to protect my younger sister.

    Soon I realized that what I was learning about family life came from a book—THE BIBLE.

6. **EVERY FACET OF THE HUMAN FAMILY WAS REPRESENTED**

    Because every part of the human family was represented in their proper relationship, I grew up well adjusted.

    A. I knew the acute discipline of a displeased father.

    B. I knew the tender understanding of an adoring mother.

    C. I had older and younger sisters and three older brothers.

    D. I knew my grandparents on both sides of the family.

    E. I knew aunts and uncles and cousins very well.

7. **A NEW FAMILY ESTABLISHED**

    When I grew up, I married and created a new family—under God. It has been a beautiful experience.

The Meaning Of Marriage
Lesson 3, Page 4

- A. From one person—myself...

  Two—with Louise...

  Our first son—Frank...

  Our second son—Stephen...

  Our third son—Peter...

- B. Then came our daughters-in-law:

  1) Carol

  2) Sue

  3) Diane

- C. Then came our grandchildren:

  1) Lester

  2) David

  3) Angela

  4) Rachelle

  5) Leslie

  6) Andrew

  7) Stephen

  8) Amber

  9) Adam

  10) Arielle

STUDY GUIDE

WORLD HARVEST SCHOOL OF CONTINUOUS LEARNING

THE WORLD FAMILY—TARGETED FOR DEATH

Lesson 4

THE THREE WORLDS OF MARRIAGE

INTRODUCTION:

Man complicates life—usually through transgression against God and the Bible.

READING:

Amos 3:3, *Can two walk together, except they be agreed?*

1. **SHOULD A CHRISTIAN MARRY AN UNBELIEVER?**

    II Corinthians 6:14-17, *Be ye not unequally yoked together with unbelievers: for what fellowship hath righteousness with unrighteousness? and what communion hath light with darkness?*

    v. 15, *And what concord hath Christ with Belial? or what part hath he that believeth with an infidel?*

    v. 16, *And what agreement hath the temple of God with idols? for ye are the temple of the living God; as God hath said, I will dwell in them, and walk in them; and I will be their God, and they shall be my people.*

    v. 17, *Wherefore come out from among them, and be ye separate, saith the Lord, and touch not the unclean thing; and I will receive you.*

2. **IF TWO UNBELIEVERS MARRY AND ONE PARTNER LATER IS CONVERTED, WHAT SHOULD HIS ATTITUDE BE TOWARD THE UNSAVED MATE?**

    I Corinthains 7:10-16, *And unto the married I command, yet not I, but the Lord, Let not the wife depart from her husband:*

    v. 11, *But if she depart, let her remain unmarried, or be reconciled to her husband: and let not the husband put away his wife.*

The Three Worlds Of Marriage
Lesson 4, Page 2

v. 12, *But to the rest speak I, not the Lord: If any brother hath a wife that believeth not, and she be pleased to dwell with him, let him not put her away.*

v. 13, *And the woman which hath an husband that believeth not, and if he be pleased to dwell with her, let her not leave him.*

v. 14, *For the unbelieving husband is sanctified by the wife, and the unbelieving wife is sanctified by the husband: else were your children unclean; but now are they holy.*

v. 15, *But if the unbelieving depart, let him depart. A brother or a sister is not under bondage in such cases: but God hath called us to peace.*

v. 16, *For what knowest thou, O wife, whether thou shalt save thy husband? or how knowest thou, O man, whether thou shalt save thy wife?*

3. **HOW LONG SHOULD A CHRISTIAN PERSEVERE IN TRYING TO WIN A MARRIAGE PARTNER TO GOD?**

   Pray and believe God for your mate's salvation until the answer comes.

   Galatians 6:9, *And let us not be weary in well doing: for in due season we shall reap, if we faint not.*

4. **WHAT ARE SOME WAYS TO WIN AN UNSAVED MARRIAGE PARTNER?**

   A. Do:
   1) Believe God for it.
   2) Claim God's promises for the entire household.
   3) Pray daily.
   4) Keep good literature to read in convenient places.
   5) Invite them to special church events—guest speakers, etc.
   6) Show a Christian attitude in love.

   B. By all means do not:
   1) Nag
   2) Keep mentioning the partner's unbelief, sins and shortcomings.
   3) Persistently beg them to go with you to church.

5. **THE THREE WORLDS OF MARRIAGE**

   I Thessalonians 5:23, *And the very God of peace sanctify you wholly; and I pray God your whole spirit and soul and body be preserved blameless unto the coming of our Lord Jesus Christ.*

The Three Worlds Of Marriage
Lesson 4, Page 3

- **A.** Spirit: When choosing a mate, the first requirement is that both flow together in the spirit. Covenant marriage has strength and stability.

- **B.** Soul: The mind, emotions and will.

- **C.** Body: Not just the body or flesh. This means who to marry. Usually you choose your companions from your church, school or neighborhood.

STUDY GUIDE

WORLD HARVEST SCHOOL OF CONTINUOUS LEARNING

THE WORLD FAMILY—TARGETED FOR DEATH

Lesson 5

THE RIGHT RELATIONSHIP BETWEEN MAN AND WOMAN

INTRODUCTION:

Woman was created by need.

- **A.** Each man needs one woman.
- **B.** Each woman needs one man.
- **C.** Woman was not made of mud, but of man.
- **D.** She was taken from near his heart to be the nearest of human relations.
- **E.** Man can choose his woman.

READING:

Genesis 2:15-16, 18, 21-23, *And the LORD God took the man, and put him into the garden of Eden to dress it and to keep it.*

v. 16, *And the LORD God commanded the man, saying, Of every tree of the garden thou mayest freely eat:*

v. 18, *And the LORD God said, It is not good that the man should be alone; I will make him an help meet for him.*

v. 21, *And the LORD God caused a deep sleep to fall upon Adam, and he slept: and he took one of his ribs and closed up the flesh instead thereof;*

v. 22, *And the rib, which the LORD God had taken from man, made he a woman, and brought her unto the man.*

v. 23, *And Adam said, This is now bone of my bones, and flesh of my flesh: she shall be called Woman, because she was taken out of Man.*

The Right Relationship Between Man and Woman
Lesson 5, Page 2

1. **WOMAN ACTUALLY RULES**

    Let each woman take her stand. The human tide adjusts to her level, whether up or down, ebb or flow. A woman is an irresistible human magnet, ranging from lowest savage to highest culture, drawing man to her level.

2. **SATAN IS AFRAID OF THE POWER OF WOMAN**

    Her concentration of hatred is turned against him. Wherever Satan's power is greatest, woman is lowest. He does not want her to vote or to get an education.

    Woman and her standing in a community is an authentic thermometer of the community's grace or disgrace.

    In some countries, wives are bought and sold as merchandise, bargained for as stock, as a necessity in building up a family tribe. On the other hand, it was woman who brought RED CROSS hospitalization to the battlefield.

    The woman's apparel, demeanor, tone of voice, carriage of body, and pervasive fragrance, are sweetening, enriching, and strengthening.

3. **WOMAN'S LOVE FLOWS DEEPER**

    Illustration: We met a woman in Paraguay who lived with her leper husband. What loyalty!

4. **CHRIST FOUND WOMAN**

    Christ found a woman in shackles, a plaything of man's pleasure, a vent to his passionate lust.

5. **WOMAN'S DEGRADATION BEGAN**

    In Genesis 4:19, Lamech was the first to take two wives, Adah (adornment) and Zillah (to hide). Lamech means "wild man." This was contrary to Eden's plan and a break from natural order. Woman's place of equality ends; she is now a female species. It was the beginning of plurality of wives, concubinage, white slavery, illicit intercourse.

6. **A WOMAN CAN BE A QUEEN OR A HARLOT**

    A. Christ's redeemed is called His Bride. A bride is holy, pure womanhood.

    B. The devil's worst is called a harlot. A harlot is a self-willed, vile person.

    C. Illustration: On a June day in London, an archbishop and a marquis went to Kensington Palace and awakened a gracious young lady from her sleep and told her she was queen.

    Queen Elizabeth ruled England well.

The Right Relationship Between Man and Woman
Lesson 5, Page 3

Oh, to awaken young ladies and tell them they are queens!

A queen in possibility can be a queen in reality, in spirit, action and choice; a queen among women in virtue and holiness.

STUDY GUIDE

WORLD HARVEST SCHOOL OF CONTINUOUS LEARNING

THE WORLD FAMILY—TARGETED FOR DEATH

Lesson 6

UNFAITHFULLY YOURS
(Hosea's Wife)

INTRODUCTION:

An unfaithful mate is one of life's greatest sorrows. Hosea wrote his autobiography when he was an older person.

Hosea was the last great prophet of the kingdom of Israel. In his historical position, he was the fourth of the Minor Prophets. He was Israel's great prophet of pathos, reminding us of Jeremiah, Judah's weeping prophet.

READING:

Hosea 6:6, *For I desired mercy, and not sacrifice; and the knowledge of God more than burnt offerings.*

Matthew 9:13, *But go ye and learn what that meaneth, I will have mercy, and not sacrifice: for I am not come to call the righteous, but sinners to repentance.*

John 3:16, *For God so loved the world, that he gave his only begotten Son, that whosoever believeth in him should not perish, but have everlasting life.*

1. **HOSEA'S PROPHECY DIVIDES INTO THREE PARTS**

    The name "Hosea" means "salvation." His wife's name, "Gomer," means "completion."

    A. The first three chapters of the Book of Hosea tell us about the prophet's private life.

    B. The fourth through twelfth chapters outline the gross iniquity of the nation of Israel at that time.

    C. The thirteenth and fourteenth chapters are an expostulation of tearful entreaties with promise of blessing to follow repentance. He wounded, then he poured in oil to heal. Hosea describes the coming judgment of God's supplication to the nation of Israel.

Unfaithfully Yours
Lesson 6, Page 2

2. **HOSEA'S BITTER DESTINY WAS TO LIVE BEFORE ISRAEL THE TRUE SPIRITUAL CONDITIONS PREVAILING IN THE NATION DURING HIS LIFE.**

   In the book of Hosea, we see the nature of sin and the nature of God's love.

   A. King Jeroboam had made Israel to sin:

   I Kings 14:16, *And he shall give Israel up because of the sins of Jeroboam, who did sin, and who made Israel to sin.*

   Israel grew more apostate, more steeped in idolatry and in infidelity to God.

   B. In Hosea's time, under Jeroboam II, they worshiped golden calves and offered pagan sacrifices in high places.

   C. Israel never had a spiritual revival after this! Backsliding is bad and sometimes it is irreparable.

3. **THE DRAMATIC LIFE OF HOSEA OPENS**

   Follow the allegory carefully between Hosea and God.

   A. Hosea received a divine call to the office of prophet. He was not a young evangelist and prophet.

   B. The prophet Hosea met a young woman named Gomer. They loved each other and were married. He discovered her to be a woman of whoredom.

   No doubt Gomer anticipated a bright, easy life. She found the parsonage lonesome with Hosea away preaching.

4. **GOMER BECOMES DISSATISFIED WITH MINISTERIAL LIFE**

   Proverbs 23:7, *For as he thinketh in his heart, so is he...*

   A. Thoughts give birth to acts. Guard your thoughts!

   B. Acts cultivate habits. Guard your acts!

   C. Habits create character. Curb bad habits!

   D. Character decides the destiny of the soul!

   Gomer grumbled, pouted and was sullen. When Hosea came home, she was miserable and non-sympathetic. The air castles of happiness burst. The home became a house. The house became a hell.

Unfaithfully Yours
Lesson 6, Page 3

5. AFTER A PERIOD OF TIME, JEZREEL WAS BORN

Jezreel means "coming judgment."

Hosea rejoiced in hope that the boy would bless the home and bring encouragement.

NO! The flaming passion for pleasure gripped the youthful woman (Gomer). The Bible says she sought after lovers and sensual indulgences (Hosea 2:7).

6. HOSEA PRAYS

God said Israel had also gone after lovers.

How horrible for a man or woman to break up a home!

7. LORUHAMAH (UNLOVED) IS BORN

   A. Gomer strays away and shows no love for her family.

   B. Town gossipers "bumble-bee" the news. Bowed in sorrow, Hosea prays. God answers the same! "Preach to my people!"

8. LOAMMI (NO KIN OF MINE) BORN

Hosea says Loammi is a child of adultery.

9. GOMER DESERTS HUSBAND, CHILDREN AND HOME FOR LOVERS

One night, one week, a month, a year, many years pass. Hosea's friends bring him the sad news that Gomer is living a life of dissipation and drunkenness.

10. HOSEA LEARNS HOW GOD FEELS ABOUT BACKSLIDING

God sorrows over sin.

11. HOSEA LEARNS GOMER IS BEING SOLD ON AN AUCTION BLOCK

Hosea runs to the town marketplace. He saw there a woman, horrible, decrepit, haggard, dirty, ragged, sad, dejected, shame-faced, bowed in disgrace—being sold at an auction.

Hosea could hardly recognize this degenerated, broken piece of human machinery.

12. HOSEA BUYS HER BACK

   A. She was sold for half the price of a slave.

   Exodus 21:32, *If the ox shall push a manservant or a maidservant; he shall give unto their master thirty shekels of silver, and the ox shall be stoned.*

Unfaithfully Yours
Lesson 6, Page 4

  B. Fifteen pieces of silver is $11.25.

  C. 1½ omer of barley (9 bushels x $4/bushel) equals $36.00.

  D. Gomer's total price was $47.25.

13. WHY DID HOSEA BUY GOMER BACK?

For home? children? ministry? No, LOVE!

14. MEETING THE CHILDREN—THE HAPPY UNITED HOME

God hates sin, but loves the sinner. The return of Gomer must have been like that of the prodigal son in Luke 15:20.

STUDY GUIDE

WORLD HARVEST SCHOOL OF CONTINUOUS LEARNING

THE WORLD FAMILY—TARGETED FOR DEATH

Lesson 7

DEMON SPIRITS BREAK UP HOMES

INTRODUCTION:

Satan has a long history of hating the home. The devil seeks to break up every home.

READING:

John 10:10, *The thief cometh not, but for to steal, and to kill, and to destroy: I am come that they might have life, and that they might have it more abundantly.*

1. **THE DEVIL TRIES TO ROB FAMILIES OF OFFSPRING**

    God's first promise was to the home.

    Genesis 1:28, *And God blessed them, and God said unto them, Be fruitful, and multiply, and replenish the earth, and subdue it: and have dominion over the fish of the sea, and over the fowl of the air, and over every living thing that moveth upon the earth.*

    A. Sarah—the devil closed her womb. God opened it when she was 90 years old.

      Genesis 17:17-19, *Then Abraham fell upon his face, and laughed, and said in his heart, Shall a child be born unto him that is an hundred years old? and shall Sarah, that is ninety years old, bear?*

      v. 18, *And Abraham said unto God, O that Ishmael might live before thee!*

      v. 19, *And God said, Sarah thy wife shall bear thee a son indeed; and thou shalt call his name Isaac: and I will establish my covenant with him for an everlasting covenant, and with his seed after him.*

    B. Rebekah was barren.

      Genesis 25:21, *And Isaac intreated the LORD for his wife, because she was barren: and the LORD was intreated of him, and Rebekah his wife conceived.*

Demon Spirits Break Up Homes
Lesson 7, Page 2

    C. Rachel was also barren.

    Genesis 29:31, *And when the LORD saw that Leah was hated, he opened her womb: but Rachel was barren.*

2. THE DEVIL IS A DESTROYER AND KILLER.

I Peter 5:8, *Be sober, be vigilant; because your adversary the devil, as a roaring lion, walketh about, seeking whom he may devour.*

    A. The devil is the source of divorce.

    Jesus said in Matthew 19:8, *He saith unto them, Moses because of the hardness of your hearts suffered you to put away your wives: but from the beginning it was not so.*

    B. Who makes hardness of the heart?

        1) Into my office come beautiful people. Young men who are strong and handsome and young women beautiful and lovely. They want a divorce. But why?

        2) I met a woman in Java who had asked a witch doctor to place a curse against her husband.

        3) I visited a home in Java where demons had thrown the wife out of the bed and would not permit her to sleep with her husband.

        4) In Rio de Janeiro, Brazil, a woman choked her husband in church. The demon in the woman hated her husband.

        5) Susie from New Mexico said the demon in her choked her husband to death.

        6) I met a man from Detroit, Michigan, who told me that while his wife looked into a candle, a demonic spirit said, "Leave your husband."

        7) In England, witches met in a conference to fast to the devil to break up every Christian home.

3. WHO DESTROYS THE HOME?

Revelation 9:1, *And they had a king over them, which is the angel of the bottomless pit, whose name, in the Hebrew tongue is Abaddon, but in the Greek tongue hath his name Apollyon.*

4. HOMOSEXUALS ARE VICTIMS OF DEMON POWER TRYING TO DESTROY HOMES AND LIVES

Romans 1:21, 26-27, *Because that, when they knew God, they glorified him not as God, neither were thankful; but became vain in their imaginations, and their foolish heart was darkened.*

Demon Spirits Break Up Homes
Lesson 7, Page 3

v. 26, For this cause God gave them up unto vile affections: for even their women did change the natural use into that which is against nature:

v. 27, And likewise also the men, leaving the natural use of the woman, burned in their lust one toward another; men with men working that which is unseemly, and receiving in themselves that recompence of their error which was meet.

5. SPIRITS OF ANGER AND FEAR CAN DESTROY FAMILIES

    A.   I was called to help a woman in South Bend who was terrified to be home alone. She would run away in the mornings to visit and shop until her husband came home from work. The marriage was on the verge of being shattered because the house was not cleaned or the dinner ready when the husband came home from work. I cast fear out of her and told her what to do. It worked, and her home was restored.

    B.   A man named Foster Colley in Laurel, Mississippi, shot his wife and himself.

    C.   Joe Mayo was shot by his father-in-law at the table during Christmas dinner.

STUDY GUIDE

WORLD HARVEST SCHOOL OF CONTINUOUS LEARNING

THE WORLD FAMILY—TARGETED FOR DEATH

Lesson 8

WHO WANTS TO DESTROY THE WORLD HOME?

INTRODUCTION:

The home is targeted for death worldwide by many adversaries.

1. **CRIME**

    Killing and robbing is a result of the undisciplined home.

2. **WOMEN ARE THE VICTIMS OF VIOLENCE AND RAPE**

    A. As common as they are disturbing, sexual assaults against women are on the rise. But they remain the most under reported cases in the criminal justice system. Every hour 16 women are confronted by rapists; a woman is raped every six minutes.

    B. Three to four million women are battered each year; every 18 seconds a woman is beaten.

    C. Three out of four women will be victims of at least one violent crime during their lifetime.

    D. More than one million women seek medical assistance for injuries caused by battering each year.

    E. The United States has a rape rate 13 times higher than Britain's, nearly 4 times higher than Germany's and more than 20 times higher than Japan's.

    F. Domestic violence against women occurs more often than incidents of rape, mugging and car accidents combined:

    1) Domestic violence   2.1 million

    2) Car accidents   522,000

Who Wants To Destroy The World Home?
Lesson 8, Page 2

       3)   Muggings   301,660

       4)   Rape   131,120

3. THE ONE-PARENT FAMILY HOME

Neither parent can wholly create a home.

4. CHILD ABUSE

Child abuse is up 300 percent. Most involve sexual molestation.

5. HOMOSEXUALISM IS LARGELY A HOME PROBLEM

6. ADULTERY

Adultery brings syphilis, AIDS and other sexually transmitted diseases as well as the breakdown of trust and love.

  A. It happens millions of times each year, but one example is a man in Florida who did not tell his wife of his venereal disease and she was infected.

  B. A woman in South Bend was married to a truck driver. He brought gonorrhea to her and she divorced him.

  C. A pastor's wife in Joliet, Illinois, took a job outside the home. He asked her not to go into the business world, but she insisted. While she was out of the home, a woman of the church came to see him. They committed adultery, and he lost the church and his home. He disappeared into the haunts of Chicago.

  D. The wife of an associate pastor in Michigan went to the church to pray. There she met a woman and became involved as a lesbian. She eventually divorced her husband.

7. WHAT DESTROYS THE HOME?

  A. Divorce

  B. Abortion

  C. Criticism

  D. Homosexuality and lesbianism

  E. Immoral television

  F. Adultery

  G. Unwed pregnancy

Who Wants To Destroy The World Home?
Lesson 8, Page 3

- **H.** Incest within the home and among in-laws
- **I.** Open marriage
- **J.** Unwed couples living together
- **K.** Pornography
- **L.** Financial disaster
- **M.** Debt—misuse of money
- **N.** Rebellious children
- **O.** The work place—both parents working

STUDY GUIDE

WORLD HARVEST SCHOOL OF CONTINUOUS LEARNING

THE WORLD FAMILY—TARGETED FOR DEATH

Lesson 9

SEVEN WOMEN AND ONE MAN

INTRODUCTION:

I was born and reared in the old-fashioned South, where puritanical ideals were exalted, cherished and rehearsed before children from infancy. In that society a woman was a lady. She was respected by men and boys; she was protected, and she was provided for. Woman was equal to man in dignity and responsibility. However, in every respect she was expected to be an example of womanliness, goodness and virtue.

In that society, one of the first things a boy learned was to esteem ladyhood.

When I was a school boy, my mother cautioned me that at all times I was the protector of my sister, a few years my junior. Sometimes this bravado attention blessed me with a black eye or a bleeding nose, but that did not deter me from insisting that my sister be respected by mischievous boys en route to and from school.

Wise and understanding men have acknowledged from time immemorial that by the all-powerful hand of woman, nations rise and fall.

It is of vital interest to the observer, how the drama of the ages has more than once spectacularly centered around the intrepid life of the team-mate God gave man almost 6,000 years ago.

One of the most significant signs in the culmination of prophecy is the place women will play in the role of history in the climaxing moments of the present age.

Today, momentous events are whirling past Father Time with stupendous velocity.

Jehovah's review of the coming cataclysm is being checked and re-checked with remarkable and indubitable accuracy.

The prophetic symbols and presaged utterances of the sacred scriptures are unfolding before a confused and bewildered world with the vividness of a superb pantomime.

Seven Women And One Man
Lesson 9, Page 2

READING:

Isaiah 4:1, *And in that day seven women shall take hold of one man, saying, We will eat our own bread, and wear our own apparel: only let us be called by thy name, to take away our reproach.*

Isaiah 24:6, *Therefore hath the curse devoured the earth, and they that dwell therein are desolate: therefore the inhabitants of the earth are burned, and few men left.*

Isaiah 13:11-13, *And I will punish the world for their evil, and the wicked for their iniquity; and I will cause the arrogancy of the proud to cease, and will lay low the haughtiness of the terrible.*

v. 12, *I will make a man more precious than fine gold; even a man than the golden wedge of Ophir.*

v. 13, *Therefore I will shake the heavens, and the earth shall remove out of her place, in the wrath of the LORD of hosts, and in the day of his fierce anger.*

1. **WOMEN'S POST-WAR WORLD**

    After any major war, the world faces a standing population of millions of husbandless women. There will be a tremendous surplus of females with no opportunity of marriage, which will represent one of the gravest international problems of history. The situation is so paramount it could alter our way of living and destroy our standards of life.

    To examine this issue, let's consult the infallible Word of God.

    Isaiah, the oratorial seer of the seventh century B.C., beheld through the telescope of prophecy some amazing trends which would develop in the endtime. Unmistakable in detail, unerring in description, the prophet predicted social and religious conditions which now exist!

2. **THE DIVINE BLUEPRINT**

    These extraordinary words dazzle the human and finite mind.

    A. A curse

    God has forecast, and it shall come to pass, a curse shall devour the earth. It is clear to my mind that the world is under a curse; at this moment it is being plagued with many evils. Civilization is devouring itself by its own ingenious devices. Modern man's super-mind has become the nemesis of his perverted soul.

    The prophet further stated: Earth dwellers are to be desolate.

    B. "Isms," "ologies" and "osophies"

    The seeing eye of the sage looked down upon a world torn with isms, ologies and osophies, marked for desolation. *The inhabitants of the earth are burned...*The globe is to be a wilderness of seared, scorched earth, as the fiery indignation fo Jehovah consumes the population.

Seven Women And One Man
Lesson 9, Page 3

C. Wars

The last clause is paralyzing, *And few men are left...* The horrible wars are to destroy the manpower of the world.

Two world wars in one generation supports the veracity of this prophecy. Millions of men, the finest in the world, are sacrificed to the angry god of war. The day approaches when few men are left!

D. Punishment

Isaiah 13, further describes the situation from Jehovah's viewpoint. *I will punish the world for their evil, and the wicked for their iniquity...* The first reading is now clearer. The curse has devoured the earth, but it is divine punishment upon a lawless, godless, evil system.

I will cause the arrogancy of the proud to cease... We must hold in mind that these amazing words were spoken to a world that had deliberately forgotten God. God declares that the arrogancy of the proud is to cease. Where is Mussolini, the Italian dictator of a generation ago, with his big jaws, big chest, big words and big empire? Where is the boastful man who would make a contract with the devil to forward his own aims and ambitions? Where is the arrogant Hitler and his screaming anathemas? Where is the Fuehrer who boasted of his Aryan race and his New Order which would last 1,000 years? They have ceased. And just so all human arrogancy will cease. God said He would *lay low the haughtiness of the terrible...*

E. Precious as gold

The following clause is one to make society tremble. *I will make a man more precious than fine gold...* Two world wars and there is greater political dilemma now than before the first world cataclysm! Calamity follows calamity depleting the manpower of the world. The day is approaching when a man will be more precious than the finest gold of the earth. Gold, the shimmering yellow god of mammon, will cease to be the standard of value, and man will be the prize. Today military strategists calculate how many men it will cost to take a certain objective—a pill box, a fortified hill, an island. They are going to become more and more cautious about throwing men into frontal attacks because reserves will be depleted.

F. The Great Tribulation

People are wondering when this judgment shall culminate: the answer is in the text. Isaiah 13:13, *...in the wrath of the LORD of hosts, and in the day of his fierce anger.* To the students of the ages, this speaks of the period of time known as the Great Tribulation, the time when the allied powers of heaven shall be in full array against the aggressive dictatorial powers of the world. God tolerated the wrath of man as long as righteous love would permit. Then when his wrath is undammed, the flood shall overwhelm man and all his works.

Seven Women And One Man
Lesson 9, Page 4

    G.   Desperate women

The last reference under consideration is a consummation. In that day of wrath and fierce anger, civilization is devoured, and the earth is left desolate and *few men are left;* the proud are humbled; the terrible lose their haughtiness, and a man becomes more precious than fine gold. In that day, seven women shall take hold of one man crying: *We will eat our own bread...* i.e. laborers, factory employees working for their own sustenance. *We will wear our own apparel...* i.e. their slacks and overalls, purchased by their own wages. They are not to be dependents, a liability, a wife. *Only let us be called by thy name to take away our reproach.* Give us your name in order to give our children legitimacy, cry the women of the last age. What a sad state of affairs when all the scruples of society are blasted to the winds and women entice men with dowries to achieve their ends!

3. THE EFFECTS OF MAN SHORTAGE

In consideration of a man shortage, to what extent have the two global wars of the twentieth century brought this about?

World War I wrought a serious man shortage when England lost one out of every 66 of her men, Germany lost one out of every 35, France lost one out of every 28!

Prior to World War II, Russia had 32 percent excess of women over men. Great Britain a 23 percent surplus female population; France, Germany and Italy had 21 to 22 percent.

Dr. Alva Myrdal, noted Swedish population expert, states that 25 percent of Sweden's women are unmarried at 40 years of age. Today Sweden's birthrate is 25 percent less than what is needed to replace the present population.

In prewar America, one out of every seven girls faced spinsterhood. Seventeen out of every 100 boys remained bachelors.

America, with the rest of the world, must face the problem of millions of husbandless women. What will be the results?

Discerning persons can see that every day of war brings the prophecy of 7 women and 1 man nearer stark reality. If the women of the world understood the times in which they live, surely they would pray to God for forgiveness of the sins of mankind, and cry to Him to bring back our men from the sanguine battlefronts of this universal war. One thing is sure, hysteria and panic will not profit; there is no merit in refusing to acknowledge this situation. Women of the world must definitely prepare to face a dark future.

4. FACING THE FACTS

One of the greatest needs of the present is to get the women of America to realize the kind of society which shall exist when there is an overwhelming shortage of potential husbands. Therefore, we shall deal with the subject from five different aspects.

Seven Women And One Man
Lesson 9, Page 5

      1) Economically

      2) Culturally

      3) Socially

      4) Morally

      5) Religiously

A. Economic effect of man shortage

Any traveled person knows that American men have raised women to almost unbelievable eminence. The rest of the world has been amazed and at times alarmed at the freedom given American women. Men of other countries say American men have set up their women as a "golden calf" to be worshiped and adored. Man plays second fiddle to his wife in the home, social life, or in business and political life. In present-day America, some women claim the right to emulate men, to run rivalry with them, rather than supplementing and complementing them.

1) Man shortage and labor

When there is a man shortage, women must do the work.

In the borders of Tibet where they have feared an excess of women for ages, I saw them used as beasts of burden, carrying merchandise strapped on their backs with horsehide across the towering mountains and wide plateaus of the hinterland. The reason was that women labor was less expensive than animal labor!

I personally visited a slave market in hinterland Asia where girls were sold for 75 cents to $7.50 U.S. currency. I have slept in "horse inns" (an overnight hostelry for travelers) where slave girls did the menial tasks. With my own eyes, I saw baby girls tied in napkins hanging in trees for vultures to devour. And there are other scenes which I do not wish to describe.

A poem written by a young American lady after hearing me speak relative to the shocking conditions of womanhood in the Orient, describes the awful plight of our Eastern sisters.

> Bound in darkest chains of night,
> Far from any ray of light,
> Steeped in sin,
> Crushed within—
> Who can make it right?
> Who can break the fettered hands?

Seven Women and One Man
Lesson 9, Page 6

> Strengthen weak and weary hands?
> Christ alone,
> Can atone—
> Free these bleeding lands.
>
> He who died on Calvary,
> Meant that these be free;
> Tell them how,
> Tell them now—
> "Jesus died for thee!"

    2)   Women of the Occident

Russia was the first European country I visited. Traveling from Japan and Manchuria through Siberia and Russia we arrived in Poland. After traveling from Java to Singapore to Hong Kong to French Indo-China, to the Tibetan border, from South to North China, to Manchuria, to Korea and Japan, we had taken it for granted that the yellow women were the bondservants of their men. However, we did not expect to see white women enslaved in Europe. I am not able to describe my horror when I saw Russian women, dressed in filthy, greasy overalls oiling the Trans Serbian Express on which I was riding. They were about the most repulsive looking white women I had witnessed—not in the least resembling what one would expect as the Mother of Civilization. We saw the women of Russia performing menial tasks from garbage tenders up. In godless Bolshevist Russia, women have been relegated to a place similar to that of pagan women. Russia was the first modern nation to have a women's army house in barracks. Womanhood is not honored in an anti-God state.

In Nazi Germany, women became the property of the State and made a slave of the State to serve the base desires of military men. Germans in Berlin told me that demonized Nazi rule had almost swept virtue out of the land. Women had become human incubators to supply material for a cruel war machine.

In every land where Christ is not supreme, woman has suffered at the hands of selfish and bigoted man. In lands which did know Christ and turned their backs upon Him, women have lost their exalted place of love and respect which God and Christ ordained she should possess.

B.   Cultural effects of man shortage

Has culture inherited from our foreparents a blackout because of existing conditions, and will the man shortage affect it?

    1)   The face of woman

When I was taken through the great Westinghouse Company in Pittsburgh, I saw greasy women wearing greasy overalls, whose greasy faces had cosmetics beneath the grime.

Seven Women And One Man
Lesson 9, Page 7

I thanked God one of them was not my mother! We are taught that the face is the mirror of character. Some analysts say that if you wish to know the character of a man, look at the face of the woman he chooses for a wife. I wonder if men would not be insulted if you told them their character could be seen in the greasy, grimy faces of women shop-workers.

2) Cuddling a machine

One thing is certain, the sweet refinements of motherhood are not found in cuddling a machine, but in cuddling a child. The breath of heaven from a mother to her child, breathed upon it all day, is what knits together the hearts of mother and child. But this is a day when many mothers are not acquainted with their own offspring. The teachings of etiquette primarily come from mother, but many of our children are growing up without proper home training. These become the gangsters and harlots of tomorrow.

3) Lost respect

A terrible aspect of this situation is that some men lose respect for working women. They dislike a woman doing the same kind of work they do. Men do not want feminine competition; men want feminine love. A man said to me recently, that if a woman dresses in the same type of clothes he wears, works in the same place he works, welds the same type of steel he welds and receives the same wages he receives, she should not expect him to stand up on a streetcar or bus and give her his seat, as he was as weary as she! This almost hostile attitude constitutes a terrible loss to women, even in their own estimation.

4) Lost prize

Culture is a prize our nation is losing in these disordered days.

C. Social effects of man shortage

Students of history have seen progressive disintegrating forces in operation to deplete and, if possible, completely destroy the home. The industrial revolution of the past century has proven to be one of the devastating forces in shattering home life. Industry has stolen the simplicity of the home, where each member lived equally around the common fireside. The domestic shop, where each member of the family contributed service, has grown into colossal chain stores and supermarkets. Interdependence in the home has turned to independence. As the youth went into other employment, parental authority and discipline were lost in the conflicting instructors outside the home. Later came mass production and with it shift work which further disrupted families. Then came two world wars smashing and breaking the homes. Fathers and husbands left to go and fight for the home they loved. While they were away, millions of mothers deliberately abandoned their homes entering public employment to be relieved of home monotony. Mothers, working all hours of the day and night, resulted in juvenile delinquency, so appalling to the legal authorities, that

Seven Women And One Man
Lesson 9, Page 8

they are unable to cope with the situation. Today, girls and boys are deeper into the gutters of crime than at any time in the history of the nation. However, not only have the youth rebelled, but women delinquency has reached a high peak. Homes are being destroyed. Divorce is mounting higher. Society is being challenged for its existence. The greater the man shortage, the greater the social disruptions.

D. Moral effects of man shortage

1) Paraguay

One of the most forceful examples for consideration is the small country of Paraguay in South America. From 1865 to 1870, Paraguay waged war with the Triple Alliance—Brazil, Uruguay and Argentina. It took three of the best equipped countries of South America six years to completely annihilate the Paraguayan Army. At the conclusion of their horrible conflict, the country was left with only 28,000 men, seven women to one man. To learn the moral results of the man shortage in Paraguay, you have but to consult any authorized book of recent date. It is estimated that from 60 - 80 percent of the population were born out of wedlock. Promiscuity has destroyed virtue and the land suffers the effects. One woman might have ten children by ten different men. John Gunther states that an army general may be the father of as many as 80 children. The children use the mother's name.

2) Japan

In Japan, the masses of men, other than Christians, are not true to their wives. They maintain that it is the privilege of men to live double standards. But the women are expected to be true to their husbands.

3) France

The moral situation in France preceding this war was calamitous. French pastors lamented the spirit of the age. Robert Ripley in his famous "Believe it or Not" asserts that Madame Jacqueline Montegaste of Paris has 17 children by 14 husbands. Polygamy in France was very prevalent before the war.

E. Religious effects of man shortage

In my travels from land to land, nothing has so intrigued me as my fellow man. Observing him under almost every circumstance possible awed me, inspired me, saddened me. In contemplating mankind, probably the position delegated to women in the universal system, is the most thought-provoking study for a traveler with a deep-rooted concern for humanity. I was constantly amazed that no matter to what extent a man degenerated, how poverty-stricken he might become, a woman was willing to be his mate and live in his squalor. In far inland Asia, I gasped to see the diseased, ragged, starving beggars, outcasts of society, living on the rubbish heaps, with their women who are faithful to them until death. In

Seven Women And One Man
Lesson 9, Page 9

modern life, a sanguine and brutal gangster who brings fear to the hearts of many, has his woman companion who is anxious to share his reckless, short-lived life. Then in Paraguay, we were horrified to find indomitably healthy women, game to enter a leper camp and live with the man she loved until death should release him from the cancerous disease. Yet in spite of woman's devotion to man, I have personally observed that in lands where Christ is not known among the masses, womanhood is not respected. In heathen and godless lands, women are made the chattels of the passions of men. For example: In Java I was present in a meeting when a man confessed that a neighbor had lost his wife in death; having no money to purchase another, he committed a great act of kindness and presented him with one of his wives free of charge!

Women have been bought, sold or given away by the whims of men.

If Christianity has a meaning, it surely means high morals, social goodness, cultural blessedness, economic security, and above all, spiritual values. Each of these has a definite relationship one with the other.

5. A MATRIARCHAL WORLD

We must assert that if wars continue as they have in this Twentieth Century, civilization will devolve to the standards of the jungles. In primitive Indian tribes, the women run the business and do the work, while the men specialize in killing. There is a possibility of producing a society where the males are human butchers, where a row of hero emblems on a modern fighter would correspond to a row of scalps on an Indian brave, which he salvaged in bloody conflict.

As America's casualty list bounds toward the million mark, some can see the "handwriting on the wall."

6. A WORD TO THE WISE

In brief, we shall sum up the inevitable repercussions resulting from an unequal sex ratio.

A. Women lowered to economic penury.

B. A definite devolution of culture.

C. The social dynamite of man shortage.

D. Lack of potential husbands results in moral debauchery.

E. Spiritual death for the community.

7. WHICH WAY OUT?

What will society do about the man shortage? Here are some possible reactions:

A. A double standard of morals. Men will be promiscuous. Society weakened by immorality and disease.

Seven Women And One Man
Lesson 9, Page 10

    B. Polygamy given a legal status. American harems will flourish. Some women already are advocating the same.

    C. Breed women as animals. Artificial insemination is successful at the present time. The idea is to take the healthiest specimens of males and breed the women.

    D. A revival of Christianity! The Bible demands that we choose. We stand responsible for the choice and the results.

    The women of America once defended their homes against savage Indians. In pioneer America, they clothed their families with garments made by their own hands. They crusaded for every good reform. But where are the torchbearers of the future? What spiritual and moral Amazon will unsheath her two-edged sword of conviction and truth and courageously wage a victorious battle against the prevalent evils of the world?

8. WOMEN OF THE WORLD

Sin is a slimy serpent that has deceived and beguiled the world! It is a ruthless monster, cruel and heartless in its devastation!

Sin has broken every ruined home, has crushed every bleeding heart, has brought wars, bloodshed and the man shortage!

Fight sin, destroy it and accept Jesus Christ as your personal Savior!

STUDY GUIDE

WORLD HARVEST SCHOOL OF CONTINUOUS LEARNING

THE WORLD FAMILY—TARGETED FOR DEATH

Lesson 10

WHAT JESUS TAUGHT CONCERNING MARRIAGE

READING:

Matthew 19:3-9, *The Pharisees also came unto him, tempting him, and saying unto him, Is it lawful for a man to put away his wife for every cause?*

v. 4, *And he answered and said unto them, Have ye not read, that he which made them at the beginning made them male and female,*

v. 5, *And said, For this cause shall a man leave father and mother, and shall cleave to his wife: and they twain shall be one flesh?*

v. 6, *Wherefore they are no more twain, but one flesh. What therefore God hath joined together, let not man put asunder.*

v. 7, *They say unto him, Why did Moses then command to give a writing of divorcement, and to put her away?*

v. 8, *He saith unto them, Moses because of the hardness of your hearts suffered you to put away your wives: but from the beginning it was not so.*

v. 9, *And I say unto you, Whosoever shall put away his wife, except it be for fornication, and shall marry another, committeth adultery: and whoso marrieth her which is put away doth commit adultery.*

1. AS IT WAS IN THE DAYS OF NOAH

There shall be marrying and divorcing and the destroying of homes.

Matthew 24:37-39, *But as the days of Noe were, so shall also the coming of the Son of man be.*

v. 38, *For as in the days that were before the flood they were eating and drinking, marrying and giving in marriage, until the day that Noe entered into the ark,*

v. 39, *And knew not until the flood came, and took them all away; so shall also the coming of the Son of man be.*

What Jesus Taught Concerning Marriage
Lesson 10, Page 2

2. AS IN THE DAYS OF LOT

Luke 17:28, *Likewise also as it was in the days of Lot; they did eat, they drank, they bought, they sold, they planted, they builded.*

Lot's wife backslid from Abraham's preaching. She married her daughters to Sodomites.

3. CHILDREN UNMANAGEABLE

Paul said that in the last days children would become unmanageable. There would be deception in the home.

II Timothy 3:1-3, *This know also, that in the last days perilous times shall come.*

v. 2, *For men shall be lovers of their own selves, covetous, boasters, proud, blasphemers, disobedient to parents, unthankful, unholy,*

v. 3, *Without natural affection, trucebreakers, false accusers, incontinent, fierce, despisers of those that are good.*

STUDY GUIDE

WORLD HARVEST SCHOOL OF CONTINUOUS LEARNING

THE WORLD FAMILY—TARGETED FOR DEATH

Lesson 11

HOW TO STAY MARRIED

READING:

Matthew 19:3-9, *The Pharisees also came unto him, tempting him, and saying unto him, Is it lawful for a man to put away his wife for every cause?*

v. 4, *And he answered and said unto them, Have ye not read, that he which made them at the beginning made them male and female,*

v. 5, *And said, For this cause shall a man leave father and mother, and shall cleave to his wife: and they twain shall be one flesh.*

v. 6, *Wherefore they are no more twain, but one flesh. What therefore God hath joined together, let not man put asunder.*

v. 7, *They say unto him, Why did Moses then command to give a writing of divorcement, and to put her away?*

v. 8, *He saith unto them, Moses because of the hardness of your hearts suffered you to put away your wives: but from the beginning it was not so.*

v. 9, *And I say unto you, Whosoever shall put away his wife, except it be for fornication, and shall marry another, committeth adultery: and whoso marrieth her which is put away doth commit adultery.*

Proverbs 5:18, *Let thy fountain be blessed: and rejoice with the wife of thy youth.*

Genesis 2:22-24, *And the rib, which the LORD God had taken from man, made he a woman, and brought her unto the man.*

v. 23, *And Adam said, This is now bone of my bones, and flesh of my flesh: she shall be called Woman, because she was taken out of Man.*

v. 24, *Therefore shall a man leave his father and his mother, and shall cleave unto his wife: and they shall be one flesh.*

I Corinthians 7:10, *And unto the married I command, yet not I, but the Lord, Let not the wife depart from her husband.*

How To Stay Married
Lesson 11, Page 2

INTRODUCTION:

Divorce is certainly one of the world's greatest problems. It is wise to take our text from the Book of Wisdom, the Bible, and from Christ, the ultimate Authority!

1. **GOD UNITED THE FIRST COUPLE**

    God created Adam and Eve and made them teammates in the Garden of Eden. It was a paradise of happiness; each served the other contentedly.

    God united the first couple. He instituted marriage. The bond was indissoluble.

    A. Satan was the first divider of husband and wife. Satan deliberately made the first family quarrel. His system of "divide and conquer" is seen here.

    B. Disobedience to God's Law brought the first family dispute.

    Genesis 3:12, *The woman whom thou gavest to be with me...*

2. **THE DISSOLUTION OF THE MARRIAGE VOWS**

    Sin is the cause of all divorce. The devil is the author. The money you spend for a marriage license can bring more happiness than any other investment.

3. **TODAY, AMERICA LEADS THE WORLD IN DIVORCE**

    Divorce is one of the chief causes of the great crime wave.

    A. Fifty states and the District of Columbia grant divorces. There are more than 65 legal grounds for divorce in the U.S.A.

    B. City divorce rate is more than twice as high as rural.

    Chicago, Illinois, grinds out hundreds of divorces a day! There are thousands of cases pending in Chicago!

4. **WHAT ARE THE ROADS TO THE DIVORCE COURT?**

    There are two aspects: 1) What the people say and 2) the real cause.

    Americans laugh too easily about divorce. It is more than hash made from domestic scraps.

    The Observer Newspaper of Charlotte, N.C., told of a Michigan wife who obtained a divorce because her husband had given each of her five step-children a saxophone!

    A. Radio and TV programs with increased emphasis on sex.

    People listen to the radio for hours and watch TV programs which glorify ungodliness, infatuation and suggestion.

How To Stay Married
Lesson 11, Page 3

- **B.** Pornographic magazines

    Half of every newsstand is filled with sex magazines destroying the fortifications of moral strength. It is not love that is being promoted, but lust.

- **C.** Movies.

    The motion picture industry has deliberately sought to damn the home. It plays the lowest morals to keep the gang out of jail. It has played divorce to the skies in fiction and real life.

- **D.** Difference of Religion

    One of the main reasons for divorce is a difference in religion or a lack of religion. The home is weakened when families do not worship together.

- **E.** Economic independence of women

    When a woman says to her husband, "I want to be independent of you," she is undermining her marriage. The man is to support his wife and take care of her. You even hear among executives where the wife works in one city and the husband works in another city and they see each other on weekends. That's the best route to the divorce court that I can imagine.

- **F.** Selfishness on both sides

    Selfishness has no place in a marriage. We are one and what's mine is yours and what's yours is mine. We flow together in protecting it and keeping it wisely as God has taught us. When you want more than you give, your marriage is in trouble.

- **G.** Lawyers wanting money

    The lawyers and judges have found divorces a very lucrative area for making money so they do not discourage it at all. They will one day give account before God for the advice and decisions that were made.

- **H.** G.I. Brides

    Girls, 15-16 years old, fall in love with soldiers in uniform and immediately they are ready for marriage. So many times, hasty marriages mean a fast move towards divorce courts.

- **I.** In-laws
    Judge: "I take it your relations are not pleasant?"

    "Mine are okay, but hers are unbearable!"

    In-laws can cause trouble in a marriage. Listen to their advice, but ultimately your home belongs to you and you alone.

- **J.** Public enemy number one—liquor!

    1) Judge Edwin M. Bobsin, Superior Court, Chicago. . ."From an examination of some 300 cases in my court, I have found that 72% of all marital difficulties were directly or indirectly attributed to liquor."

    2) Superior Court Judge, John A. Sarbaro. . ."78% of the divorce cases I have heard

How To Stay Married
Lesson 11, Page 4

       resulted from alcoholism. The deadly river of alcohol is rising and threatens to deluge American society."

    3)   90% of those petitioning for divorce say it is because of desertion or cruelty—liquor is to blame.

K.   Divorce has become fashionable—but was once a shame

The popularization of divorce by prominent persons, particularly motion picture stars, has changed the public attitude toward divorce. The American divorce rate is 50% of all marriages! Getting a hunting license takes longer than to get married by a Justice of the Peace.

5. THE AFTERMATH

  A.   300,000 orphans of living parents!

  What becomes of these children?

    1)   Judge Frank Bicek, Juvenile Court, Chicago..."70% of juvenile delinquency is a result of broken homes." (About 3,500 cases last year.)

    2)   Judge Jacob Braude in Boys' Court in 188 cities..."I found the broken home responsible for 80-90% of all juvenile delinquency."

  B.   Then they grow up

    1)   Dr. William Haines said..."65% of men and women charged with criminal offenses...have a history of divorce in their family. Many tell me they haven't seen or heard from one or both parents in years."

    2)   Dr. Louis Mann said..."A child of seven whose parents are divorced, is already on the way to divorce, even though he has never seen his future mate."

    3)   In one divorced family with 5 children:

    All went to juvenile court, one by one. One stole a bicycle, one robbed a house, one picked the pockets of a dead neighbor, and two girls ran away while in their teens to live with men out of wedlock. One now awaits the child of a married man.

    4)   Dr. Kirkendall said..."Divorce is not the answer to marital troubles. The best you can expect out of divorce is a new set of troubles."

  This is the harvest of divorce: broken hearts, suicides and murder.

  Loyalty is defeated by divorce. Betrayal is born of divorce.

6. CHRIST WANTS TO BE THE HEAD OF EVERY MARRIAGE

Christ wants to bless every marriage and be the Master of every home.

STUDY GUIDE

WORLD HARVEST SCHOOL OF CONTINUOUS LEARNING

THE WORLD FAMILY—TARGETED FOR DEATH

Lesson 12

TEN FAMILY HURDLES

READING:

II Chronicles 20:13-14, *And all Judah stood before the LORD, with their little ones, their wives, and their children.*

v. 14, *Then upon Jahaziel the son of Zechariah, the son of Benaiah, the son of Jeiel, the son of Mattaniah, a Levite of the sons of Asaph, came the spirit of the LORD in the midst of the congregation.*

INTRODUCTION:

There are very real hurdles for the man and wife for living happy ever after. They are there. They are visible. Some are high jumps—but you must win!

1. **THE FAMILY AND CHILDREN**

    An inner sanctum hurdle. The family must get along with one another, not hate one another as Isaac and Esau.

    A. The mother and the daughter.

    B. The father and the son. Every boy needs a father.

    C. Happiness must be in the home.

2. **THE FAMILY AND IN-LAWS**

    In-laws hurt many family relationships. They take sides, they add fuel to the fire.

3. **THE FAMILY WITHOUT CHILDREN**

    Families with no children can be easily broken. Adopt a child.

Ten Family Hurdles
Lesson 12, Page 2

4. **FAMILIES WITH CHILDREN FROM MORE THAN ONE MARRIAGE**

   The world has always had the problem of your children, my children and our children.

5. **THE FAMILY AND FINANCES**

   Some unavoidable financial or emotional situations demand that the wife and mother work outside the home. Perhaps there is an illness of the husband/father. This situation can cause stress or depression.

6. **THE FAMILY AT WORSHIP**

   If the family members are not all on the same spiritual level, real problems can arise as one member tries to bring the others into worship.

7. **THE FAMILY WITH A WORKING MOTHER**

   When the children are alone at home, they miss the guidance and love they need from their mother.

8. **THE FAMILY AND DIVORCE**

   A. From the very first day of your marriage, determine that you will never divorce.

   B. Pray through your difficulties.

   C. Divorce court is not for Christians.

   D. Divorce has to do with selfishness and pride.

   E. The family and remarriage.

   A remarriage is complicated because the couple often brings hurts from former marriages into the new union.

9. **THE FAMILY AND RECREATION**

   A. The family must relax together, vacation together and play together. When mom or dad are too busy, they run into marital problems.

   B. The family with emotionally-starved children, wife or husband is headed for trouble.

   C. Vacation time is not the time for drunkenness. One-fourth of all U.S. families have an alcoholic problem which undermines happiness.

10. **DRUGS AND ALCOHOLISM CAN CAUSE FAMILY PROBLEMS**

    Battered wives, abused children, automobile accidents, broken lives and divorce.

STUDY GUIDE

WORLD HARVEST SCHOOL OF CONTINUOUS LEARNING

THE WORLD FAMILY—TARGETED FOR DEATH

Lesson 13

TEN PRINCIPLES OF MARITAL BLISS

READING:

Genesis 24:58-67, *And they called Rebekah, and said unto her, Wilt thou go with this man? And she said, I will go.*

v. 59, *And they sent away Rebekah their sister, and her nurse, and Abraham's servant, and his men.*

v. 60, *And they blessed Rebekah, and said unto her, Thou art our sister, be thou the mother of thousands of millions, and let thy seed possess the gate of those which hate them.*

v. 61, *And Rebekah arose, and her damsels, and they rode upon the camels, and followed the man: and the servant took Rebekah, and went his way.*

v. 62, *And Isaac came from the way of the well Lahairoi; for he dwelt in the south country.*

v. 63, *And Isaac went out to meditate in the field at the eventide: and he lifted up his eyes, and saw, and, behold, the camels were coming.*

v. 64, *And Rebekah lifted up her eyes, and when she saw Isaac, she lighted off the camel.*

v. 65, *For she had said unto the servant, What man is this that walketh in the field to meet us? And the servant had said, It is my master: therefore she took a veil, and covered herself.*

v. 66, *And the servant told Isaac all things that he had done.*

v. 67, *And Isaac brought her into his mother Sarah's tent, and took Rebekah, and she became his wife; and he loved her: and Isaac was comforted after his mother's death.*

INTRODUCTION:

Nothing begins so happily as marriage. What happens?

Ten Principles Of Marital Bliss
Lesson 13, Page 2

1. **LEARN WHAT YOUR SPOUSE LOVES, AND GIVE IT**
    A. Coffee—black or cream or sugar?
    B. Tea—iced or hot tea?
    C. Meat—steak, fish, turkey, etc.?
    D. Colors—white, blue, red, yellow, etc.?
    E. Give it joyfully!

2. **DON'T DEMAND MORE THAN 50%**

    Man or woman, husband or wife—if you had demanded it before marriage, there would have been no wedding. Be considerate.

3. **CARE FOR THE FAMILY OF YOUR SPOUSE**

    They raised your companion!
    A. Mother-in-law
    B. Father-in-law
    C. Grandparents
    D. Grandchildren

    This does not mean that you live with them or that they live with you. It means show respect and consideration.

4. **DON'T MAKE SNIDE REMARKS ABOUT PLACE OF BIRTH, POLITICS**

    "My wife is from Arkansas. I can't get it out of her!"

5. **EXCHANGE SURPRISE GIFTS**

    This is exciting! This is love! Show appreciation for special favors.

6. **WORSHIP TOGETHER**
    A. Read the Bible and good Christian literature together.
    B. Pray together.
    C. Worship together at the same church. Enjoy the same kind of worship.

7. **VACATION TOGETHER**

    Always vacation together. It draws you closer. You have more things to talk about. When relaxing, small problems go away.

Ten Principles Of Marital Bliss
Lesson 13, Page 3

8. DON'T LET A QUARREL GET OUT OF HAND

Keep differences small. Talk a problem over, don't hide it inside.

9. CHILDREN TAKE SECOND PLACE TO SPOUSE

It is so easy for one of the parents to permit a child to assume a position of importance in the home.

The father and mother are a team. They stick together. They speak the same language to the child. They discipline together.

10. DON'T CONTRADICT EACH OTHER IN PUBLIC OR BEFORE OTHERS

This will destroy your relationship.

STUDY GUIDE

WORLD HARVEST SCHOOL OF CONTINUOUS LEARNING

THE WORLD FAMILY—TARGETED FOR DEATH

Lesson 14

DEADLY DESTROYERS OF THE WORLD HOME

READING:

I Timothy 5:14, *I will therefore that the younger women marry, bear children, guide the house, give none occasion to the adversary to speak reproachfully.*

I Peter 5:8, *Be sober, be vigilant; because your adversary the devil, as a roaring lion, walketh about, seeking whom he may devour.*

INTRODUCTION:

We do not assume to have all the answers. We have no ultimate decisions.

- A. We know that the home is the most precious of all human institutions.
- B. The devil has always hated the home.
- C. There is a daily warfare against the home. We must plan, prepare and persevere to be winners.

1. RACIAL AND RELIGIOUS DIFFERENCES

My experience in 110 countries around the world has shown that marriages which cross racial and religious boundaries are most difficult to maintain.

2. ANGER

Screaming, hitting, breaking things and having fits of rage will not promote a happy home. You can win by living in the Spirit rather than the flesh.

Galatians 5:16, 20-23, *This I say then, Walk in the Spirit, and ye shall not fulfil the lust of the flesh.*

v. 20, *Idolatry, witchcraft, hatred, variance, emulations, wrath, strife, seditions, heresies,*

v. 21, *Envyings, murders, drunkenness, revellings, and such like: of the which I tell you before, as I have also told you in time past, that they which do such things shall not inherit the kingdom of God.*

Deadly Destroyers Of The World Home
Lesson 14, Page 2

v. 22, *But the fruit of the Spirit is love, joy, peace, longsuffering, gentleness, goodness, faith,*

v. 23, *Meekness, temperance; against such there is no law.*

3. FINANCES—ONE GOVERNING ALL

The two become one, even to the point of having a common bank account. Neither should cheat financially, neither should spend without the other knowing.

4. GAMBLING

The big loser in a gambling casino is the family of the gambler. Not only do they lose their finances, they lose the husband and the father.

5. LIQUOR—ALCOHOL

Alcohol is probably the greatest family destroyer. Many people are more married to their bottles than to their spouse.

6. BAD SEX

Both must give of themselves to each other. This means being loving all day long, not just a few minutes at night.

7. LACK OF HONESTY

Never try to hide anything from your spouse. We must always be truthful and trust each other.

8. WORKING

Too long hours, especially if both are working, can turn the husband and wife into strangers under the same roof.

9. IN-LAW MEDDLING

In most divorces, the voice of in-laws can be heard.

Genesis 2:24, *Therefore shall a man leave his father and his mother, and shall cleave unto his wife: and they shall be one flesh.*

STUDY GUIDE

WORLD HARVEST SCHOOL OF CONTINUOUS LEARNING

THE WORLD FAMILY—TARGETED FOR DEATH

Lesson 15

PROTECTING YOUR HOME FROM FAMILY AND FRIENDS

READING:

Mark 6:17, 18, *For Herod himself had sent forth and laid hold upon John, and bound him in prison for Herodias' sake, his brother Philip's wife: for he had married her.*

v. 18, *For John had said unto Herod, It is not lawful for thee to have thy brother's wife.*

Luke 3:19, 20, *But Herod the tetrarch, being reproved by him for Herodias his brother Philip's wife, and for all the evils which Herod had done,*

v. 20, *Added yet this above all, that he shut up John in prison.*

INTRODUCTION:

Life has taught me that a happy home is no accident.

There are shields of protection.

Fathers should be the spiritual head of the house.

They should keep their homes clean of immorality, unbelief, and fear.

They should lead their families into spiritual power and God's anointing.

The Word of God is the key to the father's spiritual authority in the home.

1. **NEEDS FOR PROTECTION**

    We know that our homes need protection from robbers and break-ins. We have fences, some with electricity to keep out intruders, but the greatest protection needed is spiritual and moral.

2. **MORALS**

    A person who wants to do wrong can find a partner. Keep your home a private place. It will discourage:

Protecting Your Home From Family And Friends
Lesson 15, Page 2

- A. Adultery
    1) Brothers-in-law
    2) Sisters-in-law
    3) Cousins
    4) Uncles
    5) Aunts
- B. Incest
    1) Stepfather
    2) Stepmother
    3) Stepbrother
    4) Stepsister

    It is surprising how many women come to my office with regret, remorse, condemnation, depression and tears.

3. **HISTORY TEACHES US THAT MAN PROTECTS HIS HOME**
    - A. In China, very often the father picks the bride for his son.
    - B. Abraham, in the Bible, sent a servant to his family in Nahor to get a bride for Isaac (Genesis 24).
    - C. In the Near East, a stranger does not approach the tent where there are women. The women wear a veil when they are outside of their houses or tents.
    - D. In history eunuchs were used as guardians of the bed.

4. **PROTECT YOUR HOME**
    - A. No other male should live in your house, not a brother, another relative, or a friend. I know a pastor in Texas who allowed an evangelist to stay in his home and the visitor took his wife.
    - B. No other female should live in your house such as a sister-in-law, etc.

    One school teacher I knew invited her sister-in-law to stay in their home and she wound up taking her husband.

    Another woman's husband took her sister.

    In history, eunuchs were used as guardians of the bed.

    Let's protect our homes. We want you to live "happy ever after," not only in this life, but in the life to come.

STUDY GUIDE

WORLD HARVEST SCHOOL OF CONTINUOUS LEARNING

THE WORLD FAMILY—TARGETED FOR DEATH

Lesson 16

THE GREATEST MOTHER-IN-LAW

READING:

Ruth 1:1, *Now it came to pass in the days when the judges ruled, that there was a famine in the land. And a certain man of Beth-lehem-judah went to sojourn in the country of Moab, he, and his wife, and his two sons.*

INTRODUCTION:

The book of Ruth gives us a most beautiful example of the kind of commitment on which a solid family is built.

1. **ELIMELECH AND HIS WIFE, NAOMI**

    With their two sons, Mahlon and Chilion, they departed Bethlehem to live in Moab as migrators because of drought.

2. **ELIMELECH DIED**

    Elimelech died in the foreign land, leaving Naomi a widow (verse 3).

3. **MAHLON AND CHILION MARRY**

    Mahlon and Chilion married two Moab girls, Orpah and Ruth. Orpah means "double-minded." Ruth means "fullness" (verse 4).

4. **TEN YEARS**

    They lived in Moab for ten years (verse 4).

5. **MAHLON AND CHILION DIE**

    Mahlon and Chilion died, leaving a widowed mother and two widowed wives (verse 5).

The Greatest Mother-In-Law
Lesson 16, Page 2

6. RETURN TO BETHLEHEM

Naomi decided to return home to Bethlehem (verse 6).

7. NAOMI'S ADVICE TO HER DAUGHTERS-IN-LAW

Naomi urged her two daughters-in-law to remain in Moab (verse 8).

8. ORPAH

Orpah kissed Naomi and returned to her pagan and heathen people.

9. A DAUGHTER-IN-LAW CAN LOVE HER MOTHER-IN-LAW

At this point in time we observe the greatness of this mother-in-law. She showed how a daughter-in-law can love her mother-in-law.

10. RUTH, A FOREIGNER

Ruth was a foreigner to Israel. She was a Moabitess.

11. RUTH'S REARING

She was reared to be an idol worshiper.

12. COMMITMENT

Ruth made a tremendous commitment to her mother-in-law, Naomi.

13. SEVEN DECLARATIONS OF A DAUGHTER-IN-LAW

Ruth 1:15-17, *And she said, Behold, thy sister in law is gone back unto her people, and unto her gods: return thou after thy sister in law.*

v. 16, *And Ruth said, Entreat me not to leave thee, or to return from following after thee: for whither thou goest, I will go; and where thou lodgest, I will lodge: thy people shall be my people, and thy God my God:*

v. 17, *Where thou diest, will I die, and there will I be buried: the LORD do so to me, and more also, if ought but death part thee and me.*

14. RUTH CAME TO BETHLEHEM WITH NAOMI

A. How a widow won her second husband.

Ruth 3:1-11, *Then Naomi her mother in law said unto her, My daughter, shall I not seek rest for thee, that it may be well with thee?*

The Greatest Mother-In-Law
Lesson 16, Page 3

> v. 2, *And now is not Boaz of our kindred, with whose maidens thou wast? Behold, he winnoweth barley tonight in the threshingfloor.*
>
> v. 3, *Wash thyself therefore, and anoint thee, and put thy raiment upon thee, and get thee down to the floor: but make not thyself known unto the man, until he shall have done eating and drinking.*
>
> v. 4, *And it shall be, when he lieth down, that thou shalt mark the place where he shall lie, and thou shalt go in, and uncover his feet, and lay thee down; and he will tell thee what thou shalt do.*
>
> v. 5, *And she said unto her, All that thou sayest unto me I will do.*
>
> v. 6, *And she went down unto the floor, and did according to all that her mother in law bade her.*
>
> v. 7, *And when Boaz had eaten and drunk, and his heart was merry, he went to lie down at the end of the heap of corn: and she came softly, and uncovered his feet, and laid her down.*
>
> v. 8, *And it came to pass at midnight, that the man was afraid, and turned himself: and, behold, a woman lay at his feet.*
>
> v. 9, *And he said, Who art thou? And she answered, I am Ruth thine handmaid: spread therefore thy skirt over thine handmaid; for thou art a near kinsman.*
>
> v. 10, *And he said, Blessed be thou of the LORD, my daughter: for thou hast shewed more kindness in the latter end than at the beginning, inasmuch as thou followedst not young men, whether poor or rich.*
>
> v. 11, *And now, my daughter, fear not; I will do to thee all that thou requirest: for all the city of my people doth know that thou art a virtuous woman.*

    1) Ruth and Boaz (verse 2).

    2) A Moabitess of no advantage

        a) Wash thyself—as a foreigner, mourned, no children.

        b) Change thy clothes—put thy raiment upon thee.

        c) Anoint thyself.

B. Boaz observed Ruth's personality.

    1) Ruth was diligent in labor.

    2) Ruth cared for her mother-in-law. She loved!

    3) Ruth did not play around with the young men.

The Greatest Mother-In-Law
Lesson 16, Page 4

    C.   Ruth's rewards:

Ruth 4:9-17, *And Boaz said unto the elders, and unto all the people, Ye are witnesses this day, that I have bought all that was Elimelech's, and all that was Chilion's and Mahlon's, of the hand of Naomi.*

v. 10, *Moreover Ruth the Moabitess, the wife of Mahlon, have I purchased to be my wife, to raise up the name of the dead upon his inheritance, that the name of the dead be not cut off from among his brethren, and from the gate of his place: ye are witnesses this day.*

v. 11, *And all the people that were in the gate, and the elders, said, We are witnesses. The LORD make the woman that is come into thine house like Rachel and like Leah, which two did build the house of Israel: and do thou worthily in Ephratah, and be famous in Bethlehem:*

v. 12, *And let thy house be like the house of Pharez, whom Tamar bare unto Judah, of the seed which the LORD shall give thee of this young woman.*

v. 13, *So Boaz took Ruth, and she was his wife: and when he went in unto her, the LORD gave her conception, and she bare a son.*

v. 14, *And the women said unto Naomi, Blessed be the LORD, which hath not left thee this day without a kinsman, that his name may be famous in Israel.*

v. 15, *And he shall be unto thee a restorer of thy life, and a nourisher of thine old age: for thy daughter in law, which loveth thee, which is better to thee than seven sons, hath borne him.*

v. 16, *And Naomi took the child, and laid it in her bosom, and became nurse unto it.*

v. 17, *And the women her neighbours gave it a name, saying, There is a son born to Naomi; and they called his name Obed: he is the father of Jesse, the father of David.*

1)   A second husband

2)   Wealth

3)   Love

4)   A son—Jesse

5)   A grandson—David

6)   Jesus Christ was her descendent

STUDY GUIDE

WORLD HARVEST SCHOOL OF CONTINUOUS LEARNING

THE WORLD FAMILY—TARGETED FOR DEATH

Lesson 17

THE UNFAITHFUL FATHER-IN-LAW

READING:

Genesis 38:6-26,   *And Judah took a wife for Er his firstborn, whose name was Tamar.*

v. 7,   *And Er, Judah's firstborn, was wicked in the sight of the LORD; and the LORD slew him.*

v. 8,   *And Judah said unto Onan, Go in unto thy brother's wife, and marry her, and raise up seed to thy brother.*

v. 9,   *And Onan knew that the seed should not be his; and it came to pass, when he went in unto his brother's wife, that he spilled it on the ground, lest that he should give seed to his brother.*

v. 10,   *And the thing which he did displeased the LORD: wherefore he slew him also.*

v. 11,   *Then said Judah to Tamar his daughter in law, Remain a widow at thy father's house, till Shelah my son be grown: for he said, Lest peradventure he die also, as his brethren did. And Tamar went and dwelt in her father's house.*

v. 12,   *And in process of time the daughter of Shuah Judah's wife died; and Judah was comforted, and went up unto his sheepshearers to Timnath, he and his friend Hirah the Adullamite.*

v. 13,   *And it was told Tamar, saying, Behold thy father in law goeth up to Timnath to shear his sheep.*

v. 14,   *And she put her widow's garments off from her, and covered her with a veil, and wrapped herself, and sat in an open place, which is by the way to Timnath; for she saw that Shelah was grown, and she was not given unto him to wife.*

v. 15,   *When Judah saw her, he thought her to be an harlot; because she had covered her face.*

v. 16,   *And he turned unto her by the way, and said, Go to, I pray thee, let me come in unto thee; (for he knew not that she was his daughter in law.) And she said, What wilt thou give me, that thou mayest come in unto me?*

The Unfaithful Father-In-Law
Lesson 17, Page 2

v. 17,   *And he said, I will send thee a kid from the flock. And she said, Wilt thou give me a pledge, till thou send it?*

v. 18,   *And he said, What pledge shall I give thee? And she said, Thy signet, and thy bracelets, and thy staff that is in thine hand. And he gave it her, and came in unto her, and she conceived by him.*

v. 19,   *And she arose, and went away, and laid by her veil from her, and put on the garments of her widowhood.*

v. 20,   *And Judah sent the kid by the hand of his friend the Adullamite, to receive his pledge from the woman's hand: but he found her not.*

v. 21,   *Then he asked the men of that place, saying, Where is the harlot, that was openly by the way side? And they said, There was no harlot in this place.*

v. 22,   *And he returned to Judah, and said, I cannot find her; and also the men of the place said, that there was no harlot in this place.*

v. 23,   *And Judah said, Let her take it to her, lest we be shamed: behold, I sent this kid, and thou hast not found her.*

v. 24,   *And it came to pass about three months after, that it was told Judah, saying, Tamar thy daughter in law hath played the harlot; and also, behold, she is with child by whoredom. And Judah said, Bring her forth, and let her be burnt.*

v. 25,   *When she was brought forth, she sent to her father in law, saying, By the man, whose these are, am I with child: and she said, Discern, I pray thee, whose are these, the signet, and bracelets, and staff.*

v. 26,   *And Judah acknowledged them, and said, She hath been more righteous than I; because that I gave her not to Shelah my son. And he knew her again no more.*

INTRODUCTION:

Almost every young couple who gets married has a father-in-law. You may know him well, or not so well. He may be good to you or not so good. This is an amazing revelation.

Judah lied to his daughter-in-law. He became very angry that his daughter-in-law was pregnant.

She produced her evidence, pleaded her case, and won.

We must have faithfulness among all members of the family.

1. **IT ALL STARTED**

    Judah, a son of Jacob, visited Hirah, an Adullamite, or a place called Adullam. While visiting he saw a heathen girl, a Canaanite named Shuah.

The Unfaithful Father-In-Law
Lesson 17, Page 3

The Bible says in Genesis 38:2, *...he took her, and went in unto her.* He evidently married her by Adullamite custom.

v. 3, She bare a son Er.

v. 4, She bare again, Onan.

v. 5, She conceived again and bare Shelah.

v. 6, They grew up and Judah chose a wife for Er named Tamar.

v. 7, Er was wicked and the LORD slew him.

v. 8, Judah told his second son, Onan, to take Tamar, but he did not want a secondhand woman so he refused to give her a child.

v. 10, God slew Onan also.

v. 11, Judah told Tamar, his daughter-in-law, to wait for the third son, Shelah, to get older and he would give him to her.

v. 12, Judah went back to visit his friend Hirah the Adullamite. It was sheepshearing time and a time of festivities.

v. 13, Tamar was told her father-in-law was in Timnath.

v. 14, Tamar took off her widow's garments and veiled her face and sat by the side of the road as a public harlot. She observed Shelah was grown and had not been given to her as promised.

v. 15, Judah saw her, but her veil prevented him from seeing who it was.

v. 16, He begged for intercourse with a presumed harlot. He was not a young man. He had three grown sons, two of which God had destroyed because of their wickedness.

v. 16, The presumed harlot said, "How much will you give me?"

v. 17, He promised to send a goat from the flock. A good price for harlotry.

v. 17, Tamar demands a pledge of payment, a guarantee, a retainer fee.

v. 18, Tamar demanded his signet ring, some bracelets and a staff. It was a bounty.

v. 18, He agreed and lay with her. She conceived a child.

v. 19, Tamar returned to her widowhood at her father's house.

v. 20, Judah sent the goat but could not find the harlot or his pledge he had given.

v. 23, "And Judah said, Let her take it to her, lest we be shamed: behold, I sent this kid, and thou hast not found her."

The Unfaithful Father-In-Law
Lesson 17, Page 4

v. 24, Judah heard of Tamar's pregnancy. He had righteous indignation. Slaying was punishment for infidelity. Judah said, "Let her be burnt."

v. 25, As she came, she brought the signet, the bracelets and the staff to reveal the father of her unborn child.

v. 26, Judah declared her more righteous than he.

v. 28, 30, Tamar gave birth to twins.

2. LESSONS FROM JUDAH'S SIN

   A. Judah, who was Jacob's oldest son, teaches for sure that your sins will be discovered! The God of heaven has a hand in human affairs.

   B. Judah became a sinner by living with the heathen and acting like them.

   C. Judah lied to his daughter-in-law. He was immoral and wanted to kill another for the same sin.

   D. Every member of the family must be treated fairly.

STUDY GUIDE

WORLD HARVEST SCHOOL OF CONTINUOUS LEARNING

THE WORLD FAMILY—TARGETED FOR DEATH

Lesson 18

THE KING MAKES LOVE TO A STEPDAUGHTER

READING:

Mark 6:21-29,   *And when a convenient day was come, that Herod on his birthday made a supper to his lords, high captains, and chief estates of Galilee;*

v. 22,   *And when the daughter of the said Herodias came in, and danced, and pleased Herod and them that sat with him, the king said unto the damsel, Ask of me whatsoever thou wilt, and I will give it thee.*

v. 23,   *And he sware unto her, Whatsoever thou shalt ask of me, I will give it thee, unto the half of my kingdom.*

v. 24,   *And she went forth, and said unto her mother, What shall I ask? And she said, The head of John the Baptist.*

v. 25,   *And she came in straightway with haste unto the king, and asked, saying, I will that thou give me by and by in a charger the head of John the Baptist.*

v. 26,   *And the king was exceeding sorry; yet for his oath's sake, and for their sakes which sat with him, he would not reject her.*

v. 27,   *And immediately the king sent an executioner, and commanded his head to be brought: and he went and beheaded him in the prison.*

v. 28,   *And brought his head in a charger, and gave it to the damsel: and the damsel gave it to her mother.*

v. 29,   *And when his disciples heard of it, they came and took up his corpse, and laid it in a tomb.*

INTRODUCTION:

The Bible is a unique book. It commands a position over and above all other books. Its contents are such to meet the need of every temperament and personality. It has superb war tragedy; thrillers

The King Makes Love To A Stepdaughter
Lesson 18, Page 2

of heroes and villains; magnificent love stories. It has poetry of first magnitude; literature of super excellence. It has words that heal the body, cleanse the spirit and save the soul.

John the Baptist's major function in life was to institute a new regime, then turn his credentials over to another greater than he!

1. OUR DRAMA HAS FOUR LEADING CHARACTERS

   A. John the Baptist

   John was one of the greatest preachers of history, a prophet and evangelist. He was no Rev. D.D. Bishop, just John.

     1) He had rugged features, piercing eyes, flowing beard, body seared by desert sun, camel-hair suit, brawny muscles from his vitamin diet of locust and wild honey, but his sermons were not honeyed. There was no flattery in them.

     2) His sonorous penetrating voice was like a trumpet blast, awakening men from their spiritual slumber. He was no reed shaken with the wind (Matthew 11:7). His greatness was not measured by raiment or by "avois du pocs."

     3) It had been 400 years since a great teacher had come to Israel. Israel was now harassed by Roman soldiers, contaminated by Greek infiltrations, betrayed by her own priesthood! John was a voice to be heard and not seen—today seen and not heard.

     4) As John thundered his dynamic messages, like Elijah on Carmel, thousands of converts from Jerusalem, all Judea, and the region about Jordan went out to be baptized of this zealot-tempered prophet, storming the fortress of sin.

     5) John the Baptist was a type of the Holy Spirit.

   B. Antipas Herod

   Herod was a satellite of the Roman firmament, a vassal of Rome and king in Galilee.

     1) He was a son of Herod the Great, called Tetrarch, as he inherited one-fourth of his father's dominions.

     2) He was a wicked, ambitious man, voluptuous, violent, pompous and avid of riches. He did not like John, yet feared to kill him because of the people.

     3) Herod was a type of the world.

   C. Herodias the queen

     1) The former wife of King Philip, Herodias was a scheming Jezebel, a murderous Athaliah.

     2) She was a woman of the moment, a hater of good, a leader in wickedness.

The King Makes Love To A Stepdaughter
Lesson 18, Page 3

- 3) Herodias was a type of the evil one.
- D. Salome, the daughter of Herodias by Philip.
    - 1) The Bible does not give her name, but Josephus the Jewish historian does. She was a slave to her mother.
    - 2) Salome was a type of the flesh.

2. **THE PLOT OF THE STORY**
    - A. As the story opens
        - 1) John the Baptist (the Spirit) is in prison, because he had denounced the illegal union of Herod (the world) to Herodias (the evil one).
        - 2) Herod had become infatuated by his brother's wife. He wrought a separation and became subservient to her sinister influence.
        - 3) John had rebuked them and was suffering from her vindictive hatred. They arrested John and took him from the theatre under the stars and cast him in a filthy dungeon. The silver-tongued evangelist was silenced.

        These four characters are represented in each life. In many lives the spirit is bound in prison. The devil and flesh rule the world.

    - B. A banquet in an oriental ballroom.
        - 1) On some rocky cliff, we see the castle of Machaerus, a magnificent castle built by Herod the Great.
        - 2) In the banqueting hall a long table with couches is illuminated with great chandeliers and decorated with fragrant flowers. The table is laden with utensils of gold and silver. The walls are lined with trophies of war.
        - 3) The occasion is Herod's birthday. Antipas the procurator gave a great banquet for the magnates of official court, chief captains, generals, rulers, mayors, etc.
        - 4) Surrounded by luxury, pomp, pageantry, rich food, and red wine, toasts were given to the health of Herod. Ribald laughter and obscene jesting grew louder.

        No time is so fraught with danger as recreation and pleasure. When the yoke of duty is unharnessed, a person's moral restraint is lowest.

        Herod, eating delicate food and drinking strong wine, was playing with trouble. It is the same today.

    - C. An oriental custom—professional dancers were called in.

The King Makes Love To A Stepdaughter
Lesson 18, Page 4

    At the height of the feast, drunken men called for the dancers. Girls came in slightly dressed, trained in supple oriental gyrations to stir the base emotion—lust.

    1)   On this glamourous occasion, a beautiful slim youth clothed with a silk shawl slips by a stone pillar, and stands before the king.

    2)   It is 7-year-old Salome.

    3)   Herodias had sent her own daughter to dance before passion-enraged men, stirred by the monster alcohol. Many mothers in anticipation of social standing have pushed daughters too far!

  D.   Salome's debut.

    1)   It was a new step for the girl, the latest dance pantomime, her debut before the king.

    2)   Painful training taught the alluring ways to exhibit flesh to appeal to the world, by the Evil One!

    3)   Flesh will give all to captivate the affection of the world, its praise and its honor.

    4)   Salome was a sensational success in the court of Herod the King. Salome's one desire was accomplished. Sin in the First Century was the same as in the Twentieth Century.

    5)   The world offered "Flesh" whatever she desired, to half the kingdom. What is your price?

    6)   The Evil One wanted the spirit executed. A soldier was called and commissioned to decapitate John. With golden platter and broadsword, he went down the stone steps. He unlocked the door and found John praying with a light shining across his face. He cut off John's head and placed it on the gory platter with its long locks and gave it to "Flesh" who took it to the Evil One.

3.   **IS THIS THE END OF THE DRAMA?**

  A.   No! Life does not end this way. Josephus, the outstanding Jewish historian followed Herod to Rome. Prompted by ambitious Herodias, he went to Cæsar for a promotion. Bad news from Galilee turned the Roman ruler, and Herod was banished to Lugdunum in Gaul and died in exile.

    Herod could possibly see the gory head in the evening. An apparition appearing in the shadow saying, "It is not lawful for thee to have her. Repent, the kingdom of God is at hand."

    As a specter of the unseen world, John followed him. Herod thought Jesus was John.

  B.   Salome fell while dancing on ice and broke her neck. She died doing what caused the spirit's death.

The King Makes Love To A Stepdaughter
Lesson 18, Page 5

The truth is, do not execute the spirit of your life! It is God's plan for your salvation.

God had John's heart!

John did not care what happened to his head!

NOTES

STUDY GUIDE
WORLD HARVEST SCHOOL OF CONTINUOUS LEARNING

THE WORLD FAMILY—TARGETED FOR DEATH

TEST

INSTRUCTIONS: You may not use your study guide or any study notes. You may refer to your Bible but only to the Biblical text, not to the margin or footnotes, concordance, or editorial materials.

1. The institution which holds human beings in the unity of society is:
   - ☐ A. The church
   - ☐ B. The state
   - ☐ C. The home
   - ☐ D. The school

True/False
   - ☐ ☐ 2. Happiness is an achievement.
   - ☐ ☐ 3. Living happily may come by accident.
   - ☐ ☐ 4. Some people are fully prepared for divorce even before they are married.

5. God chose to bless Abraham because _____.
   - ☐ A. God knew that Abraham would keep the way of the Lord.
   - ☐ B. God knew that Abraham would teach his children to keep the way of the Lord.
   - ☐ C. Both A & B
   - ☐ D. Neither A nor B

6. The greatest disciplinary strength of a father is his _____.
   - ☐ A. Physical power.
   - ☐ B. Position as head of the house.
   - ☐ C. Ability to explain the punishment to the child.
   - ☐ D. None of the above

7. The mother's first responsibility is to her _____.
   - ☐ A. Husband
   - ☐ B. Children
   - ☐ C. Church
   - ☐ D. Job

8. Why did God create man?
   - ☐ A. As an object of His love.
   - ☐ B. As an expression of His power.
   - ☐ C. As a representative of His will.
   - ☐ D. None of the above.

The World Family Targeted For Death

Test, Page 2

9. Adam and Eve became one through _____.
   - ☐ A. Marriage
   - ☐ B. Childbearing
   - ☐ C. The fall
   - ☐ D. Redemption

10. Should a Christian marry an unbeliever?
    - ☐ A. No
    - ☐ B. Yes, in order to convert him.
    - ☐ C. Yes, if they truly love each other.
    - ☐ D. Maybe, the Bible is not exactly clear.

11. What is the proper attitude a person should take if he becomes a Christian and his spouse remains unsaved?
    - ☐ A. Separate and look for a Christian spouse.
    - ☐ B. Keep the marriage together unless the unsaved spouse leaves.
    - ☐ C. Do everything within his power to save the marriage, even if it means to deny his new faith.
    - ☐ D. None of the above.

12. How long should a Christian persevere in trying to win a marriage partner to God?
    - ☐ A. Two years is a reasonable time.
    - ☐ B. Until the unsaved spouse leaves.
    - ☐ C. Until the unsaved spouse becomes quarrelsome about the matter.
    - ☐ D. His total life

13. Which is NOT a proper way to win an unsaved spouse?
    - ☐ A. Believe God for it.
    - ☐ B. Keep good literature in convenient places.
    - ☐ C. Beg him to go to church with you.
    - ☐ D. Claim God's promises.

14. Good marriages are made in _____.
    - ☐ A. The spirit
    - ☐ B. The soul
    - ☐ C. The body
    - ☐ D. All the above

15. Satan is afraid of the power of _____.
    - ☐ A. A man
    - ☐ B. A woman
    - ☐ C. A good marriage
    - ☐ D. A good church

16. The first man to take two wives was _____.
    - ☐ A. Adam
    - ☐ B. Lamach
    - ☐ C. Laban
    - ☐ D. Abraham

Who Wants To Destroy The World home
Test, Page 3

17. Which prophet married a prostitute?
   - ☐ A. Amos
   - ☐ B. Isaiah
   - ☐ C. Hosea
   - ☐ D. Habbakuk

18. This prophet's life depicted the backsliding of the nation under king _____.
   - ☐ A. David
   - ☐ B. Rehoboam
   - ☐ C. Jeroboam
   - ☐ D. Ahab

True/False
   ☐ ☐ 19. A great revival occured shortly after the ministry of this prophet.

20. The prophet's wife was sold as a slave prostitute for _____.
   - ☐ A. About $5.00
   - ☐ B. Just above $25
   - ☐ C. Just below $50
   - ☐ D. Almost $100

21. Judah committed incest with his _____.
   - ☐ A. Mother
   - ☐ B. Daughter
   - ☐ C. Sister
   - ☐ D. Daughter-in-law

22. Herod imprisoned John the Baptist because the evangelist spoke against the king's _____.
   - ☐ A. Having his daughter dance at a party.
   - ☐ B. Marriage to his brother's wife.
   - ☐ C. Wild drinking parties.
   - ☐ D. All the above

23. The Bible prophesies that severe wars will bring the male-female ration to _____.
   - ☐ A. 1:2
   - ☐ B. 1:6
   - ☐ C. 1:7
   - ☐ D. 1:10

24. Ruth means _____.
   - ☐ A. Joyful
   - ☐ B. Double-minded
   - ☐ C. Bitter
   - ☐ D. Fullness

25. Ruth was rewarded for her love by _____.
   - ☐ A. Receiving a new husband
   - ☐ B. Receiving great wealth.
   - ☐ C. Having great men as her descendents.
   - ☐ D. All the above.

26. There are how many legal grounds for divorce in the U.S.A.?
   - ☐ A. Fifteen
   - ☐ B. Fifty
   - ☐ C. Sixty-five
   - ☐ D. Eighty-six.

The World Family Targeted For Death
Test, Page 4

27. Which of the following may lead to divorce?
    - ☐ A. Too much emphasis on sex.
    - ☐ B. Religious differences.
    - ☐ C. Economics
    - ☐ D. All the above

28. What percentage of divorces have to do with alcohol?
    - ☐ A. Less than 25%
    - ☐ B. Between 25% and 50%
    - ☐ C. Between 50% and 75%
    - ☐ D. More than 75%

29. In a study representing 188 cities, it was found that broken homes were responsible for what percentage of juvenile delinquency?
    - ☐ A. 60-70%
    - ☐ B. 70-80%
    - ☐ C. 80-90%
    - ☐ D. 90-100%

30-35. List six of the ten family hurdles:
    30. _____
    31. _____
    32. _____
    33. _____
    34. _____
    35. _____

36-40. List five of the ten principles of marital bliss:
    36. _____
    37. _____
    38. _____
    39. _____
    40. _____

41-45. List five of the deadly destroyer's to the World Home.
    41. _____
    42. _____
    43. _____
    44. _____
    45. _____

The World Family Targeted For Death
Test, Page 5

46. The home must be protected from _____.
    - ☐ A. Robbers
    - ☐ B. Immoral involvement
    - ☐ C. Spiritual decay
    - ☐ D. All the above.

Complete the following Bible verses about the home:

47. *Therefore shall a man leave his father and his mother, and shall _____ unto his wife; and they shall be one flesh.*

48. *Whoso findeth a wife findeth _____, and obtaineth favor of the Lord.*

49. *Live _____ with the wife whom thou loveth all the days of the life of thy vanity, which he hath given thee under the sun, all the days of thy vanity: for that is thy portion in this life, and in thy labour which thou takest under the sun.*

50. *Who can find a virtuous woman? for her price is far above _____.*

WORLD HARVEST SCHOOL OF CONTINUOUS LEARNING
CORRESPONDENCE COURSE INSTRUCTIONS
INDIVIDUAL STUDY

The courses offered are directed to meet the practical need of today's Christian. The following steps should be considered in beginning your study:

1. Read each lesson of the syllabus carefully.
2. Listen to the tapes carefully. They will explain the course content and clarify what you may not understand from the written lesson.
3. Read the lessons and listen to the tapes in the way most helpful to you. It is suggested you read the lesson once, listen to the tape, and then read the lesson again.
4. It is recommended that you complete each course within eight weeks.
5. At the completion of each course a test should be completed and mailed to the School so that you may earn a certificate of credit. Send $10.00 for grading costs along with your completed test.
6. You may also obtain college credit for the course you have completed by submitting a term paper on a topic related to your course. The papers should be 10 to 12 double-spaced typewritten pages. All information from source material must be properly footnoted and the sources must be listed in a bibliography. For further instruction on term paper form, please check any standard college English text book. An instruction manual on term paper writing is available from World Harvest Bible College (Box 12, South Bend, IN 46624) for $1.00 plus 50¢ postage and handling. Five source books must be used in writing the paper.

GROUP STUDY

Groups wishing to study correspondence together should have a qualified individual to teach the group. These courses can be used for pastors' studies or for home prayer and Bible study groups. It is recommended that videotape be used in the area of group study.

Further information concerning availability of materials, costs, etc., may be obtained by writing to the School.

NAME_____

ADDRESS _____

CITY_____STATE_____ZIP:_____

Name of completed course: _____

Course number _____ Date completed: _____

Mail this form, with test to:
World Harvest School of Continuous Learning
530 East Ireland Road
South Bend, Indiana 46614

For office use only:
Graded by_____Score:_____Date certificate mailed:_____

COURSES AVAILABLE ORDER FORM FOR TAPES AND SYLLABI

Send to: World Harvest School of Continuous Learning, P.O. Box 12, South Bend, IN 46624—Tel. (219) 291-3292
(All prices subject to change)

Number	Course Title	Syllabus Stock No.	Price	Audiotapes Stock No.	Price	Videotapes Stock No.	Price
T118	ALIEN ENTITIES	41023	☐$10	71043	☐$48	04300	☐$230
T128	ARMOR OF DELIVERANCE	41042	☐$ 6	71065	☐$20	06500	☐$100
T116	BATTLE FOR IMMORTALITY	41026	☐$10	71046	☐$48	04600	☐$230
T124	CHRISTIAN FOUNDATIONS	41020	☐$10	71040	☐$48	03600	☐$230
T109A	DEMONOLOGY AND DELIVERANCE I	41003	☐$10	71017	☐$48	03700	☐$240
T109B	DEMONOLOGY AND DELIVERANCE II	41011	☐$10	71035	☐$64	03000	☐$270
T112	ECSTASY	41010	☐$10	71021	☐$20	01600	☐$100
B308	EPHESIANS, LIFE IN A.D. 50	41035	☐$10	71062	☐$40	06100	☐$190
T110	FAITH	41013	☐$10	71006	☐$48	02600	☐$220
T107A	GIFTS/MINISTRIES OF THE HOLY SPIRIT I	41001	☐$10	71018	☐$48	02300	☐$230
T107B	GIFTS/MINISTRIES OF THE HOLY SPIRIT II			71019	☐$64	02390	☐$300
B304	GREAT PEOPLE OF HISTORY	41021	☐$ 6	71041	☐$52	03900	☐$260
T103A	HOW TO COPE I	41009	☐$10	71055	☐$52	05500	☐$260
T103B	HOW TO COPE II	41029	☐$10	71060	☐$52	05590	☐$260
T108	HUMAN ILLNESS AND DIVINE HEALING	41018	☐$10	71010	☐$64	04000	☐$290
M105	LIVING HAPPY EVER AFTER	41017	☐$10	71036	☐$32	03400	☐$150
T129	LOVE	41043	☐$ 6	71068	☐$44	06800	☐$210
T119	PERSON OF THE HOLY SPIRIT	41028	☐$10	71053	☐$48	05300	☐$240
T103	PERSON OF JESUS CHRIST	41034	☐$10	71059	☐$40	05700	☐$200
T113	PRAYER	41008	☐$10	71026	☐$40	01900	☐$200

PLEASE SEND FREE: ☐ ICU/WHBC Catalogue ☐ Video Extension School Catalogue ☐ LeSEA Publications Catalogue
☐ WHSCL Correspondence Course Catalogue ☐ Information on Study Tour to Israel

SHIPPING CHARGES
Orders to $10.00 .... ADD $2.00
Orders $10.01 to $25.00 .... ADD $3.00
Orders $25.01 to $50.00 .... ADD $4.00
Orders Over $50.00 .... ADD 10%

If ordering videotapes, please specify: ☐ VHS ☐ BETA

How To Write A Term Paper Manual ($1.00) .... $_____
TOTAL AMOUNT OF ABOVE ITEMS .... $_____
FOR ORDERS OUTSIDE U.S.A., ADD 35% .... $_____
INDIANA RESIDENTS ONLY, ADD 5% SALES TAX .... $_____
*SHIPPING CHARGES (see chart at left) .... $_____
TOTAL .... $_____

Name (please print) _____
Street Address _____ Tel.(____) _____
City _____ State _____ Zip _____

FOR CREDIT CARD PHONE ORDERS ONLY:
U.S.A.—1-800-621-8885
International—1-219-291-3292
Australia—08-322-1910

A SCHOOL WITH A VISION
Dr. Lester Sumrall, President
(Approved for veteran's training)

☐VISA Exp. Date _____ ☐MASTERCARD Exp. Date _____
☐A/E Exp. Date _____ ☐DISCOVERY Exp. Date _____

Indiana Christian University and **World Harvest Bible College** are charismatic schools of Bible training and ministry, plus radio and TV communications. Get an early start on your Christian education planning! Send the coupon below for a catalogue listing class schedule, financial information, admission procedure—all the main points you're interested in!

WORLD HARVEST SCHOOL OF CONTINUOUS LEARNING
Dr. Lester Sumrall Invites You To Continue Your Bible Education By:

★ **Individual Correspondence Study**

We welcome you to the exciting study of God's word through **correspondence school.** You are among a host of students studying the Word as you join World Harvest School of Continuous Learning.

The over-reaching objective of these studies is to provide a Spirit-filled practical education for those who seek to serve God in various ministries of the church or to aid those who wish to answer questions to satisfy deeper longings for a fuller understanding of God's Word. It is our intent that our students will be equipped to properly interpret and expound the Word of God and exercise the gifts of the Spirit so that many souls may be brought into the Kingdom.

Students around the world are able to participate in the life-changing courses presented by Dr. Lester Sumrall by following the lectures on **audiotape** and the accompanying point-by-point **study syllabus**. There are over 50 presently in print. For your convience there is an alphabetized syllabi reference and order form on the other side of this page.

★ **Video Extension Studies**

Church and home groups as well as college classes join in the powerful yet practical lectures from Bible-based how-to-live classes. The videotapes enable the groups to have **Dr. Lester Sumrall** as their guest teacher each class session. There are over 60 topics available and each videotape contains 2 - ½ hour lessons.

★ **Study Tour To Israel**

LeSEA Tours are not just sightseeing tours, they are educational adventures with uplifting and inspiring moments of meditation. The Christ-centered charismatic studies right on the spot where these earthshaking events happened, are spiritually rewarding. It will add a new **dimension** to your Bible reading and you can receive three hours college credit if you fulfill the requirements.

While in the Holy Land you will stay in top deluxe hotels with all meals included in the price.

Dr. Lester Sumrall has visited Jerusalem more than fifty times and has lived there with his family. He will share with you the spiritual significance of this magnificent land, its history, the prophecies that have been fulfilled, and yet to be fulfilled. You will be enriched by his knowledge of prophecy, history and keen biblical insights.

★ **World Harvest Bible College**

A residence college situated right in the middle of LeSEA's worldwide ministry headquarters. WHBC trains young men and women in the latest technology of mass media and evangelism. WHBC offers A.A. and B.A. degrees as well as a one-year certificate in Christian Ministry. WHBC is approved for the training of veterans and international students.

Please send me:

☐ Correspondence catalogue ☐ Video extension information ☐ Holy Land tour brochure ☐ WHBC catalogue
Ministries please include your tax number to give our Auditing Department backup for your trade discount. Make checks payable to LeSEA Publishing.